Marching to a Different Tune

of related interest

The ADHD Handbook
A Guide for Parents and Professionals
Alison Munden and Jon Arcelus
ISBN 1 85302 756 1

Attention Deficit/Hyperactivity Disorder
A Multidisciplinary Approach
Henryk Holowenko
ISBN 1 85302 741 3

Pretending to be Normal
Living with Asperger's Syndrome
Liane Holliday Willey
Foreword by Tony Attwood
ISBN 1 85302 749 9

From Thoughts to Obsessions
Obsessive Compulsive Disorder in Children and Adolescents
Per Hove Thomsen
ISBN 1 85302 721 9

Asperger's Syndrome
A Guide for Parents and Professionals
Tony Attwood
Foreword by Lorna Wing
ISBN 1 85302 577 1

Marching to a Different Tune
Diary About an ADHD Boy

Jacky Fletcher

Jessica Kingsley Publishers
London and Philadelphia

First published in the United Kingdom in 1999 by

Jessica Kingsley Publishers Ltd,
116 Pentonville Road, London
N1 9JB, England

and

325 Chestnut Street,
Philadelphia, PA 19106, USA.

www.jkp.com

© Copyright 1999 Jacky Fletcher

Author's note
All names have been changed, including that of the author, to preserve confidentiality

Library of Congress Cataloging in Publication Data
A CIP catalog record for this book is available from the Library of Congress

British Library Cataloguing in Publication Data
A CIP catalogue record for this book is available from the British Library

ISBN 1 85302 810 X

Printed and Bound in Great Britain by
Athenaeum Press, Gateshead, Tyne and Wear

To my children – each one special and unique, and to Stefan especially, without whom there would be no story to share. To my husband and to all my family who are so supportive and loving.

Contents

Preface

I have covered four years of extracts of life with Stefan, our son who has ADHD or Attention Deficit Hyperactivity Disorder. My diary may give some insight into what it is like living with a child with ADHD. From the moment he was born, we knew he was different. He slept very little, and seemed only to cat-nap. I was lucky if I got a two hour stretch at a time when he slept, day or night. He seemed unusually alert, with his little eyes darting everywhere, taking everything in.

Nothing prepared us for a child like him. By the time he was three, he was displaying many of the characteristics typical of ADHD although at that point we had never heard of any such disorder. Unlike our daughter, he did not respond to and seemed impervious to any form of discipline. At nursery school he did not seem to fit in with the other children and spent his time flitting from one activity to another and displaying increasingly anti-social tendencies.

We became more concerned, especially as he continued not to need much sleep. By the time he reached school age we were being constantly criticised even though I knew there was something wrong, something I could not put my finger on. Despite our attempts to train him, he seemed to have no bottom line. We felt embarrassed, guilty and confused.

By the time he was six, he was receiving one to one help all day at school as his behaviour was so impulsive and unpredictable that he could not be trusted on his own for a minute. He had already flung a plastic bin lid at a child, knocking her tooth out, to the parents' fury. He had to come home for lunch every day as the school were not able to accommodate him during this time, although they were admirable in providing all the extra help that he so obviously needed. We took Stefan to our GP who referred us to child guidance. This achieved very little and so a return visit to our GP saw him referring us to a specialist and from there to Great Ormond Street where he was diagnosed as having a severe form of ADHD.

My initial reaction was one of relief, that our hunches much earlier on in his life had been correct and that there was a genuine reason for the way that he was. Then I went through a night of real grief, because I realised that we had a child who would require such careful handling and training and patience and wisdom and that he may never be as other children. I would have to learn to develop a thick skin and a sense of humour. Sometimes people could be cruel and thoughtless and critical. I joined a support group and learned as much as I could about the disorder and explained to family and friends and those with whom he came into contact and found that people became more understanding although it did not lessen the disruption that he could cause both inside and outside the home.

He still requires an enormous amount of attention and mental energy, often driving us to the point of exhaustion. He is mischievous, fun-loving, can be charming and has a winsome personality with a wonderful sense of humour. He is talented in many areas, sensitive and artistic and despite his poor concentration and poor self-regulation so apparent in children with ADHD he is an intelligent and enterprising boy. My husband Vaughan and I love Stefan and our two girls very deeply and we are committed to helping him in any way we can to enable him to reach his potential. We are Christians who love God and believe that His son Jesus Christ came into this world to save us all and that He has a plan and purpose for Stefan's life and so we pray for him daily that he will be helped and that we too will be given the strength day to day to cope with whatever the day brings forth. It is not easy and it is often extremely challenging and exhausting. But we are always hopeful and always we care and endeavour to do our parenting job the best we can.

I see parenting as a great privilege and resp-onsibility, and our children as wonderful and unique gifts to us. Having Stefan has maybe helped round off some of the rough edges in us and made us more understanding towards those who struggle to raise a child who has difficulties. We thank God for giving Stefan to us. He is very special. He marches to a different tune.

1995

This boy – tomorrow's man
Catch him – if you can
Tousled blond hair – azure eyes
Skids 'cross the floor as around you he flies

Sense of danger – no fear
Warnings – often doesn't hear
Smiles at an old tramp in the street
Chats to anyone he may meet

Unreserved – he'll give a hug
Heartstrings – he knows how to tug
Large limpid eyes – innocently
Blinks amazed – 'What…me?'

Life is lived at double speed
Not much sleep does he need
Exhausting, interesting – likes to annoy
Complicated – loveable boy

February 21st

Stefan is ten today! There were times when we wondered whether he would reach ten with his dare-devil antics and accident record. Anybody with an ADHD child will know what we mean.

He awoke at 3am muttering 'It's my birthday today.' I hushed him up and told him that it was the middle of the night. He woke again at 5am and wanted to get up. I heard him opening a present we had left for him. At 6am he was whizzing around. He opened the door of our bedroom and I told him '7 o'clock please and not before'. After that I didn't sleep again as he was too noisy and he bounded in at 6.45am rousing the whole family with renderings of 'Happy birthday to me'.

It's hard to believe he is ten in some ways – he seems so much younger. We had had a job to find four friends to come to his roller skating party and then in the end only two turned up. How often my heart aches for him when other kids let him down. That evening we took him out for a meal – just our little family. He just could not sit still. He darted about asking questions, touching the restaurant's model trains and handling everything. The manager did not like his constant questions and movements, we could tell by his face. Fortunately, we were the only ones there!

March 1st

Stefan belongs to a swimming club and at early morning training today there was an upset. He had smuggled a penknife into his sports bag (he often smuggles things from home into school or some other place). The other boys got to know about it in a short time and came out of the changing rooms talking about 'Stefan's penknife'. One of the dads who dislikes

Stefan made loud protests. Some of the mums tried to be supportive to me, but the dad spouted off about how inconvenient it was having a child like Stefan in the club, and eventually I walked away from him because I was getting too upset.

So many times in the past there have been similar scenarios with criticism aimed at us or Stefan. I have never learned to be that thick skinned. I cried for a long while. That evening a phone call came from the chairman of the club saying that reluctantly he would have to suspend Stefan from the club for a week until a committee meeting had taken place.

March 8th

The chairman of the club rang and dropped a bombshell. According to a unanimous vote by some of the parents, Stefan was to be suspended permanently from the club. I was so shocked and choked up that I could hardly speak to the man. He said he had done his best to put the case in Stefan's favour, but the parents wanted him out. Both his swimming teachers, not part of the committee, were cross at the outcome as they had worked hard with Stefan and had learnt to adapt their teaching methods somewhat, finding him very responsive. We had tried to encourage his swimming, it is something he does well and we had been advised by the specialists dealing with Stefan to 'channel his energies'. We had no idea how we were going to tell him.

March 9th

Stefan looks forward to his swimming club nights and mentioned it today. I had to tell him of the decision. He was devastated. 'Why aren't I wanted? No-one wants me', and he proceeded to reel off the places he had not lasted at: Judo, football training, tennis lessons, gym club and boy's brigade. His self-esteem went down another notch.

March 14th

Stefan has a fascination for matches. Today he filled an old sock with paper and sprayed my antiperspirant all over it and said he was going to set it alight – his bomb! Thank goodness I found it in time!

March 25th

This morning Stefan managed to fall right through a plate glass door at home whilst we were in bed, trying to have a bit of a lie-in. His face was so badly gashed that we had to rush him to casualty which is about four miles away. He had to be stitched up by a facial surgeon. Poor little thing. I felt so sorry for him as he lay on the huge couch squeezing my hand hard as the injections were given to numb his face. He talked incessantly even during the injection, and at one point told the surgeon 'When you've finished sticking that needle into me I'm going to put it right through your backside!' We were advised to try and keep him fairly quiet for the rest of the day. What a joke! Ever tried keeping an ADHD child *QUIET* !

Within minutes of arriving home he was running around and showing everyone his stitches. When I took him to the library to choose a video to hire, he found a ready audience and graphically explained all the gory details of his 'operation' to poor unsuspecting old ladies, librarians or anyone else, talking louder and louder in animated tones, until I grabbed a video and almost dragged him outside.

His last accident occurred whilst playing around a swimming pool on holiday last year in Turkey, when he split open the back of his head. He had to be taken by ambulance to a private hospital to be stitched up. Two years ago, he stepped on to our ceramic cooker hob which was on and sustained a burnt foot which necessitated a visit to casualty. He has burnt his leg on an iron, and has had to have over forty splinters removed at once when he crawled through a tiny gap in a fence. He has fallen against a table and gashed the corner of his eyebrow, just missing his eye when he was belting round it, and has had butterfly stitches put in his head after falling from a post he was trying to climb during yet another holiday.

April

After Stefan was asked to leave his swimming club, I left it for a while before making enquiries about another one. After several phone calls to various people, I found a local club who were willing to take him. I told them exactly how he was, covering up nothing, but they seemed undeterred and assured me they would be able to cope. I hardly dared to raise my hopes even when they said they had dealt with many children with special needs in the past. We went. Stefan was assigned to a class with a lady to take special charge of him if needed. He began the session by pushing a child into the water from the poolside. He could not wait his turn in the queue when the children were lined up to swim one at a time, alternating between pushing in front of others, refusing to go into the water when it was his turn, picking up equipment on the poolside or generally jumping, fidgeting or climbing on everything.

From the spectators' gallery I sat in embarrassed silence – an all too familiar pattern. Some mothers watching showed looks of utter disapproval. I turned round and tried to speak to a couple of women who looked a bit kinder than the rest. 'He has a slight disability – um – he's – er – hyperactive with an attention deficit disorder – um – he – er – can't really help it!' I half apologised. 'Oh, it's a shame isn't it?' one of them sympathetically replied. 'Well it's embarrassing too,' I explained. We chatted for a few moments more.

After the sessions I asked the swimming instructor, 'Well, what do you think? I really understand if you think that you won't be able to accommodate him, but I would rather know now than let him get involved to be told at a later date that he is not able to continue. It would be very detrimental to him.' 'It's okay, we will be able to cope,' I was assured. 'We won't get rid of him but we shall be very firm with him.' 'That's fine,' I agreed, and I promised to let them have a fact sheet about his condition to help them understand. Stefan is a very good swimmer and I was so glad to have another opportunity for him to join this club.

April 20th

Stefan went out for the day to a local country park where some organised activities were taking place. I had a quiet word with the organisers in case he became disruptive, which he often does when there are a lot of other children around in an informal setting. I gave him his medication before setting off and we picked up another little boy to go with him. I love him so much, but it was a nice break and things returned to normal for a day with my two daughters and me left at home. After the activity day, Stefan had been reasonably all right, so we brought the other little boy home with us to play in the garden for an hour. Everything went well, until, without warning, Stefan filled a bucket of water and tipped it all over the child, drenching him from head to foot. Fortunately he had a change of clothes in his bag from the activity session and, being a particularly mild-mannered boy, accepted Stefan's behaviour in a good-natured way.

At bed time, Stefan nicked some food out of the fridge for lunches the next day. He frequently takes food from the fridge, cupboards and particularly our freezer. It is almost an obsession. Often I make a batch of scones, biscuits or cakes if I am expecting visitors. By the time my visitors arrive, my freezer containers are nearly always devoid of goodies. It is infuriating. We have admonished, pleaded, punished, begged – all to no avail whatsoever. Our accusations are always met with a strong denial even when the evidence is found in his bed, or bin of crumbs or cake cases. Eventually, perhaps the next day, he admits his guilty deed. We have tried buying boxes of biscuit crackers, extra fruit, and giving him his own little corner of a cupboard for his own snacks, or allowing him to make peanut butter sandwiches for supper, but still things go missing.

He seems to crave sweet things. One day I had made some rich chocolate mousses and placed them in four individual dessert dishes ready for some dinner guests. They were carefully placed in the freezer. To my horror, when I came to get them out, someone's finger had left deep indentations across two of the dishes rendering them useless to serve to our guests! I have had to buy a padlock and lock certain things away in a cupboard. Other items that have to be kept in the freezer are now transferred to my sister's freezer. It is a good thing that she only lives about four hundred yards from our house. Stefan soon discovered my padlocked cupboard. Not to be deterred, he unbent a wire coat hanger and laboriously fed it through a tiny gap in the double doors until he managed to hook it on to a box of cookies balancing on a shelf – and yes – somehow devoured the lot!

April 30th

It began as a bad day. Stefan and his dad clashed badly and Stefan managed to do lots of things to irritate him. The final straw came when I saw Stefan rushing up the stairs with my husband in hot pursuit, telling him to get into his bedroom. I wondered what had gone wrong this time. 'WRONG?' yelled my husband. 'HE'S ABSEILING DOWN THE HOUSE.' It must have been the wild glaring eyes, or the flaring nostrils or the way he said it, but I saw the funny side immediately and turned to hide a smile. At least it partly diffused the situation and I mean, if one does not have a sense of humour sometimes, I think we would all be taken away by little men in white coats!

May 2nd

Stefan punched a boy in the mouth at school today, after the child insulted him. He kicked several others. He has shown aggressive behaviour lately. We usually find that if a child has made fun of him or knocked his already fragile self-esteem, that Stefan will always take revenge, usually with an aggressive reaction. Although we must have told him thousands of times that this is inappropriate, he seems to forget when faced with a confrontational situation.

May 3rd

Stefan disappeared for an hour today. When he came home he seemed surprised at my concern. 'I was only playing with my friend,' he reasoned.

Stefan is not allowed to go around the neighbourhood on his own, even though he is ten, because of his unpredictable behaviour. He has been found cycling up the middle of the road, or weaving in and out of parked cars before now with little or no sense of any danger, so he has quite close boundaries and is only allowed to ride his bike on the pavement. But it is harder now he is older to be always watching him and yet we want to be able to start trusting him.

May 4th

Stefan decided to go off again. It was an hour and a half today. I drove around the streets looking for him, anxious, my mind conjuring up all sorts of things. Eventually he phoned from a friend's house down the road. I grounded him for a week.

May 8th

Down at the beach there were many families milling about, with children playing happily. It was warm and sunny – VE day. My husband was working, so I took the three children to the old town where there were bands playing and crowds jostling along the seafront. It was not long before the children met up with friends from their schools, and we were playing together on the sands. Stefan started to climb up ropes and a ladder that was nearby, balancing on a very narrow ledge with a sheer drop of about ten metres the other side, unconcerned and unaware of any danger. I knew my son. If I approached him he would inevitably try to escape, further endangering himself. I sat where I was, calling. The more I called and warned him of the danger, the more he seemed to enjoy my and everyone else's reaction. I had to try to pretend to ignore him until he eventually climbed down. I could almost hear the sighs of relief resounding in the air from those who had been watching. Some little Chinese boys were playing nearby. Stefan pulled his eyes into slits mimicking them. It was time to go!

We drove to Southend. I had to buy some things for my oldest daughter. I dread shopping with Stefan but this time I had no choice. In British Home Stores he picked up the dummies modelling the children's wear. Next he jumped on to a dummy stand, posing next to one, not batting an eyelid. When a poor unsuspecting couple walked by he jumped out at them. They almost died of fright. Next he ran up and down the escalators – the wrong way – or played with the electronic cash tills, messing them up. Just as the poor harassed looking cashier appeared, he put his arms around her waist and hugged her. Then he was off again, rushing around the store, banging between the clothes stands, knocking clothes flying whilst emitting loud noises of his voice. My head wound up tighter and tighter until I felt I would burst with frustration and anger.

That evening, I cut Stefan's hair. It was like dealing with an eel. He fidgeted and moaned non-stop until I was accidentally cutting zig zags in his hair. I got cross. As he lay fast asleep and curled up in his bed that night with his blond tousled head so peacefully on his pillow I felt so sorry for getting angry with him.

May 10th

One day a week, for just over an hour, a carer comes in to look after Stefan so that I can either be with the two girls, or do some shopping in the supermarket. I really appreciate this short time although he poses quite a challenge to the carer. This particular day they went for a walk. On the way home, Stefan decided to knock at a friend's door. The family were out. He went round to the back garden – when he did not reappear after a few minutes, the carer went round to find him. There he was, in their shed, happily sorting it out for them!

May 16th

If Stefan gets an idea into his head, it can quickly become an obsession. He decided he wanted a budgerigar. I explained that it was impractical to keep a bird with two cats and a dog. Besides, they were enough to cope with. He began to go on about it. He even begged an old hamster cage from a neighbour and cut out a model of a budgie from cardboard, placing it inside the cage. He talked about having a real one all the time, asking the cost of a bird, cage, food, and so on. Every time we stopped at the pet shop to pick up stuff for the other pets, he went to have a look at the budgies and begged me to buy him one. He does not easily accept 'no' for an answer and can get into quite a bad temper, kicking things, hitting out at the girls and saying how much he hates us all.

May 20th

My husband and I were going out to relatives for a meal. It is such a task trying to fix up baby-sitters. Because Stefan is one person's work, we usually find that it is better to send the girls to my mum's or my sister's for the night and have someone in just for him.

Other times we have asked a baby-sitter to come in for the girls as there are two local families whom we know well who will occasionally have Stefan overnight. By the time I have sorted out overnight things and got them and myself ready I have sometimes wondered whether it was worth it!

May 24th

It does not matter how good Stefan is being, or whereabouts he is in the house, as soon as I get on the telephone, he appears from nowhere and proceeds to talk loudly, act clownishly, open cupboards and get things out, or generally behave in a disruptive attention-seeking manner. Tonight was no exception. A friend called me on the phone and, true to form, Stefan appeared from nowhere and began his antics. This time he decided to get my egg slicer out of the kitchen drawer to see what he could slice up in it. First he tried some paper. Then a carrot, and then his finger. I chatted to Sam keeping a watchful eye on Stefan. Suddenly he pulled down his pyjama trousers and placed a certain part of his anatomy into the egg slicer. I quickly shouted at him to remove it and suddenly realised what I was yelling down the phone to the poor unsuspecting caller. Was my face red!

June 9th

Stefan was chosen to represent the school in the Borough swimming gala next month. What an honour! I felt glad that at least he would be able to train a bit, at his swimming club. But when we arrived that night, we were told 'Sorry, but Stefan cannot continue here, it is too difficult to cope'. I suppose the word 'devastation' would be the right one to use for how both Stefan and I felt.

June 10th

Jane, Stefan's oldest sister, is almost twelve. She finds Stefan a constant embarrassment in front of her friends. Sometimes he spits on them and uses bad language, or else he is jumping on top of them or looking up their skirts. She has little privacy as he is always barging into her bedroom and taking her things. We fixed a lock on the door, but after many kicks and beatings, the door finally gave way. The furniture in his own bedroom is nearly all broken and his toys never last long. The other day he smashed up his attractive wall clock. He has slashed his melamine units with a knife and pulled out cane sticks from a cane bookcase, to make a bow and arrow with. He has pulled the sides off his bunk bed and destroyed most of his possessions. He has even cut holes in his new pyjamas.

June 12th

Stefan had a particularly bad day at school, punching and hitting other children. My heart sank when he came out at home time, escorted by the deputy head teacher. I was aware of the other mums around me all watching, and I felt the all-too-familiar feelings of humiliation and embarrassment creeping up. The school wondered, had he taken his medication that morning, because it seemed as though he had not. He had been wild and aggressive. Stefan takes a Ritalin tablet soon after he wakes up in the morning. Usually first thing he is extremely hyperactive, rushing around all over the place, jumping on beds, furniture and acting mostly without thinking. After taking his medication, within the hour there is a noticeable difference and a calmness comes over him. He becomes more sensible, thoughtful and quieter.

Occasionally, for some unknown reason, the tablets do not seem to have any effect on him. He takes another at midday, at school, but often during the course of the afternoon his teacher notices his concentration levels falling. He has an optional third tablet after school, but often we are loath to give him this one as we have found that it can affect his sleep. Without this one he goes to bed at a reasonable time, though often not actually sleeping until later. With the third tablet we have on many occasions found him still awake between eleven and midnight.

Stefan asked recently why he had to go to Great Ormond Street Hospital. 'Am I handicapped?' he wanted to know. I tried to quickly think of an appropriate answer. 'Well, Stef, everybody has a handicap of some sort – something that spoils their life a little.' 'Like Daddy – he has a *golf* handicap, doesn't he?' Stefan said. 'Well, not quite like that.' 'What's your handicap then, Mummy?' he wanted to know. 'I get headaches a lot, that's mine. They would spoil my life a bit, sort of interfere with my being able to get on, so sometimes when I get one, I have to take a tablet and it helps it get better.' 'What's Louise's then?' (his youngest sister). 'She is quite a fearful little girl, isn't she?' 'What's mine, then?' 'Well,' I continued, 'you have a bit of a problem concentrating and sometimes you do things without thinking of what might happen. Your tablets help you with these things, that's all.' He seemed quite satisfied with this reply and dropped the subject. We feel that, for Stefan, if he were told at this stage in his life that he has ADHD, he will easily become a victim and probably play on the knowledge, making easy excuses to opt out of developing responsibility for himself or his behaviour.

June 20th

Stefan's latest trick in any shop we go into is to lie flat on the floor looking under all the counters, stands or other appliances for any stray coins. He has gathered several pounds through this new business enterprise. When I have managed to pluck him up from this position, in the middle of a shop usually, I make him go to the shop assistants and tell them where he found the coins. Usually he receives a pat on the head and a smile saying 'Well now, how honest of you to tell me. You may keep the coins'. Stefan often takes money from my purse or Vaughan's drawer by his bed. When questioned, he fiercely denies any knowledge of the missing money.

He always seems so plausible but unfortunately he is given to lying about many things. It often seems that he mixes fantasy with reality. He tells teachers things like 'My mum's gone away for a long holiday' or he comes home with stories such as 'We're having a re-designed playground built at school. There is going to be an adventure playground, a pet's corner, trees and a sports area'. I guess this vivid imagination and wishful thinking takes over from the basic truth, which is that the playground would be undergoing a facelift.

June 25th

Wherever we go, Stefan seems to attract trouble. Children will be playing happily together until he comes along. He seems to goad others. Despite being sensitive when other children taunt him he can be incredibly insensitive towards others, calling them names and being extremely rude. Whether we go to the park for picnics or to the beach, trouble arises. One day recently in the park, he saw two boys about his own age, playing on their bikes, minding their own business. He began to taunt them, calling out 'Fireman Sam, Postman Pat'. Soon the boys got fed up and they began to follow Stefan, looking aggressively towards him. Because Stefan was with a friend, he put on an act of bravado and continued to taunt from a distance, until I saw fit to leave the park.

Another day on the beach he began to throw stones at a group of boys in the water. I have to intervene delicately enough not to completely humiliate him in front of peer groups, yet to let him know that his behaviour is unacceptable. I do not often feel I can fully relax on such occasions but always I need to be vigilant, keeping a watchful eye on him.

June 27th

We went to the beach and Stefan took a friend. I sent the two boys to the kiosk to get an ice-cream each. They were gone for ages even though the kiosk was only about one hundred yards away. I went to look for them after a while, and met them coming back. A tall hedge separated the pathway from a bowls green.

Suddenly an elderly lady's voice could be heard clearly from the other side of the hedge. 'How dare you throw stones over on to the green, you naughty children.' One look at the boys' faces told me all I needed to know. I told them to go and sit on the beach whilst I continued quickly to the kiosk to get my youngest an ice-cream as promised. When I returned, they had disappeared. 'They've gone out to the creek, over the mud flats,' my oldest daughter told me, 'in their school shoes.'

June 28th

Whilst Stefan's carer was with him, Stefan decided to visit the attic. Our loft ladder was broken but he somehow managed to gain footholds over the drawer units on the landing and swing himself up. Although very slightly built, he has strong arms and legs. He found a suitcase packed full of old family photographs in glass frames. In usual Stefan manner – acting before thinking – he dropped the suitcase, some nine feet, onto the landing. Needless to say, about thirty family photo frames were smashed into smithereens that day.

June 29th

A picnic after school in the park. Stefan disappeared for about ten minutes. He returned trailed by a group of four boys on bikes. They told me he had found some matches and had set light to a bin full of waste paper.

June 30th

A weekend trip to a holiday site in Kent where we rent my sister's chalet each year. Stefan always tours the site on arrival, checking to see who is there and quickly making himself known. He visits everyone's chalet, whether he is welcome or not, and constantly asks about their lives, where they come from and for how long they are staying. People either love him or find him something of a nuisance. He is unreservedly affectionate towards all, often catching people unawares by flinging his arms around them and hugging them tightly. I suppose he could be called 'a loveable rogue'!

July 1st

I thought that I would trust Stefan to go to the indoor swimming pool on the site, about fifty metres away. I figured he could not get up to much mischief as there were so few people around that weekend.

Will I never learn? After a short time he appeared, dripping wet, with the manager by his side. My heart sank. What now? The manager reassured me that there was nothing to worry about, but he wondered, could my little boy by any chance have moved a pair of very expensive spectacles belonging to an elderly gentleman from the changing room? Quite likely, I thought to myself. The manager went on to say that although Stefan and the gentleman seemed to be the only ones in the pool, Stefan had denied all knowledge of any spectacles and had told the manager he had seen a couple of youths larking around in the vicinity.

Trying hard not to knock his already fragile self-esteem, I said aloud, 'OK, Stefan, I want you to go down to the pool with the manager and help him look for those glasses, you're good at finding things – and don't come back until they're found, right?' Off he went, whistling. A little later he returned looking pleased with himself. 'I found them for him. Somebody had stuffed them down the air vent in the changing room.' I asked him who he thought it was. 'Those boys,' he replied. 'It certainly wasn't me, Mum.' I let it drop.

On the way home, some hours later, Stefan turned to me in the car. 'I did it.' 'What?' 'Put that man's glasses in the air vent.' 'Why?' I asked. 'Because I was messing about in the water, and the manager came and got me out. That silly old man swimming about was muttering "What a naughty boy, what a naughty boy...", so I decided to get back at him.' I explained that if he had damaged the glasses we could have got into a lot of trouble. I don't know how much he took in.

Came home from shopping to find Stefan, who had been left in the charge of his carer for an hour, at the end of our driveway, with our dog on a lead and a box by his side and a concertina being 'played' collecting money for Great Ormond Street. He had even collected a few pounds! The next day, he and a friend, both of whom attend the hospital in question, went up and down our road unbeknown to both sets of parents, knocking on every door stating 'We're collecting money for Great Ormond Street. We are hyperactive and we are patients there. Please give some money!'

In all, the pair of them collected thirty pounds. Before any of it could be 'accidentally' pocketed, I took it and wrote out a cheque for the amount. My husband and I explained why they could not go collecting either on their own or without an official box but nevertheless they showed enterprise and so we praised them for their effort. I sat with Stefan whilst he wrote an accompanying letter and we sent the money off. He was pleased to receive a personal acknowledgement and thanks a few days later.

July 7th

Stefan did not know I was watching him through the kitchen window. He threw objects over the fence into our neighbour's garden. Then in a loud audible voice he was heard to say to the dog, 'Pepsi, you mustn't do that!'

Stefan has always been extremely alert. Even as a tiny baby his eyes would roam the room, taking everything in. He sees things the majority of people miss. His alertness, if channelled right, could be a great asset. This particular evening about a dozen children were playing outside our local swimming pool. Not one of them noticed a thief hovering about the area. He got out a pair of pliers and clipped a bike chain holding two bikes together, and rode away quickly on one of them.

Stefan, who was with the children, saw it all happen and ran inside the pool entrance to tell me. My first thought, I have to admit, was – another of Stefan's fantasies. But the look of consternation and urgency on his face was enough to convince me otherwise. I rang the local police station and within five minutes a police car and two uniformed officers arrived on the scene. Stefan was able to give them a fairly detailed description of the man and the evidence was there – one severed bike chain. The bike belonged to one of the lads who was swimming at the time. The officers thanked Stefan for his alertness. He was our little hero that day.

July 12th

More good things! Stefan swam for his school in the Borough Gala and gained a certificate of merit and first placement in the boys' relay race. He then gained a silver medal for breaststroke. Oh how we glowed with pride that day!

July 14th

Somehow Stefan's medication was overlooked this morning. Did the school know about it?! According to his teacher, there was absolute chaos in the classroom. He climbed on top of a high cupboard and proceeded to do a dance to the class. He ran about jumping on and in everything, and was very wild. Not a good day.

August 8th

Stefan was awake early. Before the rest of us were up, he found a box of matches and made himself a little fire in his bedroom basin. I could tell by this early action that we were in for one of those BAD days. The previous day he had been really good most of the time, but today he was fidgety, restless and excitable. As my daughters were both out at activities, I took him to McDonalds on his own for lunch. He ate fast and furiously, as though he were about to catch a train, stuffing food into his mouth, not waiting to finish each mouthful despite my corrections.

Afterwards we had to go to the supermarket. He grabbed a trolley and whizzed up and down the aisles nearly knocking two toddlers out of their buggies and barging into people. I grabbed him as he sailed past, scooting on the back of the trolley. I severely reprimanded him and took his trolley away. Five minutes later he appeared with another trolley. I took it off him. He helped himself to a can of drink and downed it quickly. As I got to the check-out feeling frazzled and weary, I noticed Stefan had disappeared yet again. A security guard came over, with Stefan in tow. What had he done *this* time? Horrors! He had found a razor and tried to shave a little boy's arm and had cut him. The mother was understandably cross. I made Stefan apologise and once again also apologised for my child's inappropriate behaviour.

August 10th

Stefan turned the hosepipe on my youngest daughter, Louise, drenching her. He then decided to hose the poor long-suffering dog. It reminded me of when he was about four. One day the hosepipe was in the garden. Stefan turned the tap full on, picked up the hose and stood in the doorway leading in from the garden and proceeded to water our dining room from top to bottom, furniture and all!

Another time when he was about the same age we had a young girl to help look after the children for a few months. One day Stefan shut her inside the shed whilst she was fetching something and when she tried to get out, he turned the hose full pelt on to the door, thus preventing her. The poor girl was trapped for some time with Stefan laughing with glee, until I realised what was happening and went to her rescue!

August 11th

Stefan smuggled a large crab home from the beach. Later on, my oldest daughter told me had had thrown it onto a passing car in our road. The cars move slowly up our road as we have speed humps. Stefan often places various objects in the road and watches with delight as the unsuspecting cars grind their way through them. One day my husband found him sitting on a plastic chair right in the middle of the road. Another time he decided to lie down in the middle. His guardian angel must work overtime!

August 12th

I was lying on our local beach, soaking up some sun with Stefan beside me. Suddenly he jumped up and went over to an elderly lady sitting a few yards away and gave her an enormous hug. She looked flabbergasted at first and I felt a little embarrassed. I wonder what goes through Stefan's mind. Did he think she looked lonely and in need of some affection?

A few days later I was standing in the newsagents waiting to be served. A lot of people were passing in and out. Again without warning, Stefan suddenly darted over to a middle-aged lady and flung his arms around her. I thought it might be someone from his school whom I did not know. I asked her 'Does my son know you?' Recovering from the shock she replied 'No dear'. 'I'm very affectionate!' chortled Stefan, as the poor lady muttered an embarrassed 'Oh, how sweet…!' and hurried out of the shop. Stefan has always been fairly free with his affections and displays little inhibition regardless of who the person may be. He seems to get along best with the elderly or the very young.

The summer holidays are now almost over. During the weeks of hot days and endless sunshine we usually went down to the beach with a picnic after hurrying through the necessary chores first thing. I bought an inflatable dinghy and oars and Stefan spent many hours rowing around in it very adeptly. Or the children would get engrossed in 'crabbing' with their nets, buckets or crab-lines when the tide was out. There was always something for them to do. There were intermittent clashes with other children on the beach, with Stefan usually right in the centre of any trouble, and often leading to mud slinging or stone throwing and feuds until I hobbled over the stones bare footed, to quickly intervene. Once or twice other mums came over and complained about what Stefan had done, but after apologies and a short chat it was generally settled amicably.

Yes, it has been a good summer holiday. I had planned the days and activities, and because the weather was so good we were able to be out of doors each day which made it so much easier. Stefan is going to be in his last year at Junior School when he goes back. It will be hard to get back into routine. I have enjoyed the six weeks school holidays. I always look forward to them, despite the difficulties, and feel quite sad when they are over for another year.

September 6th

Back to school. Peace reigns! Stefan has a very nice teacher who seems so cool, calm and collected and always seems to have a smile on her face. Oh dear!

September 13th

Stefan has been busy making a 'shop' on our dining table. He turned the home upside-down in the search for things to sell. He and his younger sister arranged the items neatly, with labels to mark the prices. Then they stood at the end of our driveway lying in wait for passers-by. Not one person was allowed to escape from the sales patter that he delivered and the majority were press-ganged into our home to at least view the trinkets and paraphernalia. Some of them were obliging enough to buy one or two items, after which they were allowed to leave. This 'shop' continues every day after school for several days until the novelty has worn off. Stefan would make a good salesman.

September 14th

Today Stefan worked out that if he stuffed tissues up the bubble-gum machine near our house, then the bubble-gum would not drop down when people put their money in. Later he would extract the gum for himself.

September 15th

Stefan got hold of his older sister's alarm clock. He drowned it in her bedroom sink.

September 16th

A new den was on Stefan's agenda for today. He emptied everything out of the garden shed and swept it out. Small tables, desks and chairs mysteriously disappeared from the house, along with toys and books and games and even a rug. For the next couple of hours he and Louise were absorbed in cleaning, sorting and arranging the items in the new 'home'. Then an hour of peace followed when all three children sat in their finished 'pièce de résistance' playing board games and enjoying the fruit of their labours.

September 20th

Another complaint from a mum today. Apparently Stefan had hit her little boy in the school playground. I made Stefan apologise and explained to the mum about Stefan. She was not that interested.

Had a locksmith in to put a lock on Jane's bedroom door as Stefan keeps going in and taking her things.

September 21st

Stefan used bad language to a class helper. He had to write a note of apology.

September 22nd

Conker season! Stefan knows all the haunts where the conkers are and every day after school we have to trek around with plastic bags to collect them in. I am becoming quite an expert at swiping at the trees with long pieces of wood with Stefan egging me on to 'hit harder'. He has collected hundreds but it is never enough. When the novelty has worn off, they will be laid to waste all over the house, in bags, or in corners, or stuffed in coat pockets.

September 23rd

Stefan is usually up first in the morning. Lately we have found him out in the garden at about seven thirty, roller skating at top speed up and down his home-made ramps. Not far from where we live is a skateboarding place where the ramps are built at varying levels, some extremely high. The kids go there with skateboards, skates or bikes and whizz up and down. Many of them are real experts at performing leaps and tricky manoeuvres. Stefan loves to go there on his skates and is fast becoming quite adept at tackling some of the ramps. He seems not to mind when he takes a tumble or skids on his backside.

October 1st

During the morning service at church, Stefan was fiddling about, playing with the sash of my pinafore dress behind my back. I ignored him, thinking at least he was being fairly good. I soon realised why – he had tied my sash to my arms!

October 4th

Told Stefan to go up to bed. A while later I found him in the bath wearing his swimming trunks, snorkel and flippers. All my pretty miniature soaps were in the bath too, and he was 'diving' for them.

October 8th

Vaughan took him to the skating ramps. He threw pieces of wood in front of the skaters nearly causing an accident. Vaughan brought him home.

October 9th

Took the children to an autumn fayre. He made a pot on a pottery wheel. When we arrived home he found the play-dough and wet it all down. He then splodged it on the turntable of his record player in his bedroom. As the turntable spun after being switched on, I found him trying to make pots!

October 10th

Stefan's music lesson went dreadfully today. His teacher said not to bother to bring him next week if he was like it again. I realised I had not given him a 'ritalin' tablet before the lesson.

October 15th

I was so pleased when I glanced at Stefan sitting quietly in the church pew this morning. He seemed to be colouring in a picture. He was – with my Tippex! He also superglued two fingers together.

After a bath this evening, Stefan shot downstairs. After only a minute or two I rushed down after him when I heard him in the kitchen. In that short time he had managed to open the fridge door, take two eggs and chuck them into a neighbour's garden. The neighbour shortly arrived at our front door to ask if Stefan had done it. Stefan denied all knowledge and I stupidly thought he could not have done anything so quickly. Need I say more?

October 16th

The craze at school this term is milk caps (pogs). Stefan helped himself to his older sister's pogs and sold them at school and at the end of our driveway, and earned five pounds. He denied that he had taken them and said they had all been his. I decided to really try to handle this without losing my 'cool'. As Stefan got into the bath I went and sat with him. I explained how we all did wrong things when kids and then lie to try to cover up. 'But I didn't take them,' he insisted. I explained how Jane felt, that she had built up a collection and now it was ruined. I told him I loved him ever so much and would think a lot of him if he could put it right and that it was not nice to benefit from someone else's loss – it was how burgling starts. 'Oh poor Stef-Stef,' he said. (This is his way of admitting his 'crime'.)

I asked him how he thought he could put it right. 'Give her half the money,' he suggested. We called Jane into the bathroom. Stefan apologised to her and offered her half of his ill-gotten gain. 'It wouldn't buy me what you've taken,' she said. 'OK, ALL my money,' Stefan wailed. I reminded him that it was ill-gotten. Later Jane came into his bedroom. 'I've been thinking – I don't want to make a profit out of this, I only want to replace what you took. Here's a pound back, Stefan.' Everyone was happy.

October 17th

Stefan helped himself to my 'Christmas' drawer and took my wrapping paper and a whole roll of coloured tape. Yesterday's lesson was forgotten for the meantime. I sometimes almost despair, but I am determined not to give up. He also taught himself how to pick a padlock with a bent wire coat hanger.

We are decorating our lounge at the moment. Stefan got in when we were not looking and emulsioned half a wall. Luckily the new wallpaper had not been put on!

October 21st

Sam phoned. Stefan appeared from nowhere as predicted. This time he had managed to burst a plastic football and had torn it into many pieces. He had the pieces hanging out of his sleeves, collar, socks, shoes and pockets. He got the egg slicer out. I grabbed it QUICKLY!

October 27th

Stefan was cross because I had told him off. He rushed upstairs and pulled his shirt buttons off.

October 29th

Stefan sprinkled itching powder down a five-year-old's back.

October 30th

Stefan climbed out on to the garage roof and sprinkled the contents of a tin of talcum powder all over our driveway.

October 31st

Stefan wanted to go 'trick or treating'. We do not permit our children to do this, and so I suggested an alternative. He wanted a few fireworks, so we bought some rockets and set them off in the garden with the family. Later on, he escaped from the house, all dressed up in fancy dress. Apparently he went around the neighbours' houses demanding: 'GOD OR JESUS?'

November 1st

He made a concoction of talcum powder and water. Then he got hold of the bleach and mixed it with half a bottle of disinfectant. Some of the bleach spilled onto our newish bathroom carpet. I also found a bottle of almond essence empty!

November 2nd

Stefan came home from school and disappeared upstairs. He reappeared some time later and proudly showed me his 'tattoos'. My black eye-liner pencil was used up along with my red freezer marker!

November 3rd

The school have implemented a target system for Stefan. He is set his targets for the day and rewarded with stickers if he manages to meet them. At home, the stickers are exchanged for plastic 'chips' which are collected and strung up in his bedroom. He may either trade a few in for a small reward or accumulate them for larger treats. He is quite enthusiastic about this at the moment.

November 4th

We arrived at Sam's house after an annual general meeting. Stefan ran amok, opening cupboards, drawers, touching things and rushing around like a mad thing. He wanted to let off fireworks. He ran into the pub next door to 'help' let some off. At ten o'clock when we were about to leave, Stefan was missing. After a short search we found him sitting in Sam's bath in the warm water, his clothes strewn all over the bathroom. Talk about make yourself at home!

November 6th

Stefan smashed a light bulb and sat picking all the little bits of glass from it. Why? Why does he do anything?

November 7th

Today he managed to break the whole light fitting in his bedroom. We had to get an electrician in.

He unravelled a whole tape cassette.

I gave him a 'ritalin' tablet quite late in the afternoon. Disaster! He was awake until a quarter past midnight, tipping his room upside-down. He tied string around his bunk bed and sellotaped a chair to his bed and took his mattress off his bed. Finally he fell asleep in the midst of the chaos.

November 8th

With my help, his room was put back to rights. After school he demolished one stereo speaker that was in his bedroom, and turned his room upside-down again.

November 9th

Stefan pinched eggs from my kitchen. He broke a bit from the top of each one to empty the contents and filled them with water. He threw them at Vaughan and Jane as they came up the stairs.

November 10th

Today a film crew arrived. They were to film Stefan as part of a programme to be screened about attention deficit disorder. We were not to give Stefan his medication until later on that day. Well, they asked for it! He ran and jumped and swirled and bounced and threw himself about AND on to them and kept them all busy. Later on, when he had received his medication the film crew remarked on the striking contrast. Stefan took great delight in showing them his bedroom – the holes cut in his pyjamas, the bleached T-shirt, the slashed lampshade, the dart holes in the walls, the wax marks on his table from melting candles, the burn marks in his basin from his bonfire, the bedroom units with knife marks sawn into them and the writing on his bed with Tippex. Stefan hugged the two female members of the crew many times. It was an interesting day.

November 11th

Horrendous weekend! Stefan was completely 'over the top' – running, jumping, hitting out, throwing himself about. I felt worn to a frazzle and I am ashamed to say I snapped and really yelled at all of the children and then ended up crying myself!

November 13th

Stefan came home from school with a certificate for good behaviour today. Obviously he had worked it all out of his system over the weekend. His teacher said he had been an 'angel'!

November 14th

We are on to yet another new idea – this time it is a BAR! Stefan found some empty wine bottles and beer cans and filled them with Ribena (thank goodness that was all!). He extracted all our wine glasses from our cabinet and arranged them along his shelves. He took our cocktail mats and carried extra chairs up to his room. He changed his light bulb to a soft red glow bulb and arranged the seats and cushions. He placed a notice on his door 'The King's Pub' and urged his dad and me to 'come to my pub'. For a family which does not frequent pubs and bars I would love to know where he got the idea from!

November 15th

Stefan has become obsessed with collecting old bottles and filling them up with water or Ribena for his 'bar'. He has now written a cocktail menu:

Iced water
Water
Ribena
Ribena and water

Every caller to our house is press-ganged into having a drink at 'The King's Pub'. (For a small payment, of course!)

November 16th

I have noticed my face creams and perfumes seem to be vanishing rather quickly, along with yet another tin of talcum powder, bleach, bubble bath, shampoos and disinfectant. It is costing a bomb! Perhaps he's making them!

November 20th

The 'pub' interest has waned and it is on to new things! Like Robin Hood. A friend lent him a video of the film and Stefan assumed the role after watching it. He made a bow and arrows. They were ingeniously put together complete with feathers on the arrows. The bow and arrows were made from my once-prized wicker bookcase and no doubt some poor little bird is sitting naked without its feathers!

December 2nd

Our next door neighbour knocked on our door. He said that something not very pleasant had been thrown from our bathroom window upstairs, on to his side passageway. Could we please make sure it did not happen again? I was aghast and embarrassed to say the least, and did not have to think twice to know who the culprit was. Of course it was immediately denied. Nevertheless he was made to write a note of apology. It went like this:

'Dear Pete (*name changed*), My mum and dad say I've got to write and say sorry for something I did not do or they'll smack me to death.'

Vaughan was so cross and screwed it up and threw it away. 'Write it properly,' he ordered. Two more notes followed in similar fashion and each one Vaughan threw away until finally a short simple note was delivered next door with a personal visit from Vaughan to assure the neighbours it would never happen again. Stefan eventually owned up.

Took the children Christmas shopping. Stefan wanted his Christmas money to spend. We entered a shop where I handed him a pound with instructions not to leave the shop. A few moments later he rushed up to me proudly scrunching a paper bag. 'I've got Dad's present,' he announced. 'Now I need to get yours. Can I have another pound?' Off he went again. This happened four times in all until his money ran out. 'I've done my Christmas shopping,' he declared.

That night we discovered he had bought two penknives. We confiscated them immediately and explained why he could not have knives. He was so cross. We reminded him that we had warned him on numerous occasions about having knives. 'You could even be expelled from school if you were ever found to have one on you,' explained Vaughan. We also reminded him of the stabbing incident on the news recently.

December 10th

Our home was quite peaceful for a change on this particular day, when there came a knock on the front door. Our neighbour stood there glowering. Our hearts sank. What now? 'What's Stefan got about our side passageway?' he wanted to know. SHAVING FOAM all over it and down his side window. Vaughan told me later that he had seldom felt so embarrassed especially after assuring our neighbours that Stefan would not be throwing things out of the bathroom window again. It transpired that he had been playing with his dad's shaving foam, shaken it up and then *punctured* the can with a knife, a most dangerous thing to do, as Vaughan pointed out to him, which could so easily have resulted in dire consequences. When the foam oozed out all over the place Stefan said he thought he would get into trouble if it went all over the bathroom (which it was anyway) so he threw it out of the window!

December 12th

When we arrived at school today, I was greeted by the deputy and head teacher. 'Did you know that Stefan brought two penknives into school yesterday?' she enquired. 'He couldn't have, his dad threw them away,' I replied. I was shown them. Identical. My brain clicked into place. At only one pound each, he had purchased *four* on Saturday when he had seemingly been buying presents.

December 13th

We have noticed two 'FOR SALE' signs go up – one on either side of us!

1996

February 21st

He's reached ELEVEN!

March 10th

Stefan has discovered that the large tree across the road from our house is good for swinging on. He swings out deliberately in front of passing cars as the tree is right on the edge of the pavement. P.S. Thank goodness there are speed bumps in our road!

March 13th

Stefan had his desk moved at school. He subsequently tore up a lot of his school work including his project book for the term and the whole of his maths book. On Open Day we had very little work to view!

March 14th

He hung his bike from the upstairs landing banisters with a piece of rope and left it dangling in mid-air.

March 15th

Stefan somehow managed to get into the box that I keep hidden with suitable snacks for the children's lunch boxes. Most of the crisps, snacks, etc. were eaten. It had been padlocked!

March 24th

I keep my sister's key to her house on my key ring. Stefan took it off one day and went up to her house whilst they were out. He looked around and helped himself to peanuts in the cupboard. He also ate a whole handful of chocolates that were on her sideboard in a box and then shifted things around. She thought she had been burgled.

March 25th

He phoned up Buckingham Palace and asked to speak to the Queen.

March 26th

Tried to phone 10 Downing Street and talk to John Major! No luck, so he phoned a random number and left a message on an answer machine to ring back. Stefan answered when he called back and asked this man if he had children. The man said, 'yes, why?' Stefan then asked the man if his children would join a club he was starting up and left the man with the details about his club. I should think the gentleman concerned was flummoxed!

March 27th

Stefan found an adapter lead for his tape recorder and cut off the end to make a 'Swirly Thing' that he had seen on TV. End of useful lead.

March 28th

Outside school, an irate mum caught up with me. She told me to tell Stefan not to rip her daughter's clothing. Stefan said it had been an accident and they had been playing. He tends to get the blame even if he does something unintentionally.

March 29th

Received a telephone call from another parent. Would Stefan please stop ringing her daughter, sometimes up to four times in an evening. She said Stefan also pestered her daughter at school and the child was fed up with his obsession for her. I apologised and explained that we have more than one phone in the house and he was obviously calling from the upstairs one.

March 30th

I was chatting to my next door neighbour – she mentioned that eggs were found in her garden. Now I wonder who that could have been?

March 31st

Stefan is constantly being told not to eat food with his fingers, especially Shreddies and soft boiled eggs!

April 2nd

Dear child put a dart through his bedroom window. He also threw a dart repeatedly at his wooden desk causing the wood to splinter all over.

April 3rd

Smashed his plastic hockey stick over and over on the pavement outside our house until it was in little pieces.

April 4th

In our local library Stefan found a chair with wheels. (Why didn't they hide it when they saw him coming?!) He wheeled himself around all the shelves as fast as he could with me in hot and embarrassed pursuit!

April 6th

Stefan crash landed on my sister and brother-in-law's patio table, completely smashing it. I had to replace it for them at a cost of twenty-seven pounds. (Who says we don't need DLA (Disability Living Allowance)?)

April 16th

He threw talcum powder all over the bathroom.

April 17th

I discovered radiator fluid leaking all over Stefan's bedroom carpet. I found many little holes punctured into the radiators. Darts had been thrown. The result a new radiator costing seventy-five pounds with fittings. Darts confiscated for good.

April 19th

Stefan tried to take his bike to bits to make a unicycle. We visited the chiropodist. Stefan climbed onto the chair, got hold of the controls and shifted the chair as high as it would go. The chiropodist and I could not reach him. Suddenly he rushed off the chair and into an adjoining room surprising a doctor and a nurse!

April 22nd

Threw a tomato at a neighbour's little boy.

April 23rd

Called in to school. I was told that Stefan's behaviour had become worse lately. He was being rude to members of staff, running round the school building and hiding in various places. His target system did not seem to be working whereby he gained points on completion of his work and generally was lacking in interest.

April 30th

Stefan took and passed Grade Two piano exam.

May 1st

Stefan stopped all the escalators whilst we were in a large department store in Southend.

May 18th

Stefan and his friend packed a suitcase full of dressing up clothes, toys and make up and other items and disappeared to our local village for over an hour. Found out that they had entertained shoppers and passers by with a display of 'circus tricks', having dressed up in the clothes and painted their faces with my make-up. Apparently they collected two pounds which they promptly spent in the nearby newsagent. Stefan bought a hundred penny chews!

May 20th

His class teacher told me that he took a huge bite out of his English Book.

May 21st

Vaughan looked everywhere for Stefan's school packed lunch which had been put out ready the night before, next to his sisters' lunches. He was in a hurry so they had to leave without finding it and pay for a school dinner. Stefan later confessed to having eaten it the night before.

May 27th

Just completed the emulsioning of our landing and hallway walls. The little chap threw a satsuma up the stairs at his sister and it splattered all down the fresh new paint.

July 10th

Vaughan and I attended an Educational Tribunal in London to oppose the local education authority's decision not to statement Stefan (that is, to provide funding and extra resources for a child with special needs). We had a three hour hearing. We felt confident that we would be successful with our appeal. The members of the tribunal were surprised that as yet a secondary school had not been allocated for Stefan.

July 19th

School's out for summer! Stefan missed the last three days as he was unwell, a rare occurrence. He was not able to say goodbye to all his teachers and the other children. The end of primary school.

July 20th

Stefan recovered enough to go on a Crusader holiday in Wiltshire. This is his first real holiday away from us alone. The Crusader team were well informed about

Stefan and ADHD. Have sent a little information (not *too* much!) and they seem happy to have him. Took him to the camp and promised I would keep in touch with them throughout the week. Felt a bit choked up when I waved him goodbye.

July 21st–23rd

Missing Stefan.

July 24th

Vaughan received a phone call from the Crusader camp. They had had enough – would Vaughan go and fetch him home. Apparently, amongst other things, Stefan had tried to climb out of an upper bedroom window. He had taken a sword from the wall and messed about with it and also removed all the safety gadgets from every fire extinguisher in the school where they were staying! Vaughan managed to appease the and persuaded them to persevere until Saturday. They agreed. He had a strong 'fatherly' talk with Stefan.

July 26th

I hear that we have been successful with our appeal. Stefan is to be re-assessed for statementing. We still have not found a school that will accept him. I am not going to let it worry me enough to spoil the summer holidays.

July 27th

The Crusader team deserve a medal! They managed to survive the week! Drove down to Wiltshire to collect him. Although he turns our lives upside-down, we really missed him. Could not wait to see him again. Got some funny looks when I arrived. Found out why later. Stefan had told members of the team that 'mum's a prostitute and dad's a jockey'!

July 28th

Back to chaos.

August 14th

Stefan went for a bike ride – *inside* Iceland freezer shop.

August 15th

Covered himself with deodorant – all over the outside of his clothes.

August 17th

Vaughan and I took Stefan and Louise to London and visited the Science Museum after Stefan's appointment at Great Ormond Street. He ran amok. He saw some nude models in the human biology department and ran around singing as loud as he possibly could. Vaughan thoroughly embarrassed and disgruntled and the day ruined as nearly all our times out together end up.

August 20th

Stefan catapulted a stone out of the car window.

August 21st

Our beloved dog, Pepsi, was run over by a bus today. The whole family was devastated. Stefan did not show a great deal of emotion until later that evening, when he was in bed. He became angry. He was angry at God for letting it happen, angry at the bus driver and angry at the vet who had to put her down because her spinal cord was severed. He was a very sad little boy that night.

August 22nd

Stefan does nothing but talk about getting another dog. Despite Vaughan's and my obvious grief, he seems oblivious to it. At night he changes, and cries for Pepsi. During the day he goes on and on about another dog for him.

August 26th

Yes, we've all succumbed! We have got a new dog – 'Mad' Molly! She is big, boisterous and completely dotty (so are we). I feel sure that if it were possible for a dog to have ADHD then she would be that dog! We are so busy looking after her, (trying) to train her and make her feel at home that she has taken our minds away from our grief over Pepsi, somewhat.

August 28th

Throughout the holidays, at regular intervals, I have been chasing up schools, education departments and even written to our local MP about Stefan's situation of no school for him to start in September. It seems we are no nearer to a solution.

September 4th

The children returned to school after summer break. Stefan is still at home. No news.

September 10th

Still no news about a school. I am implementing a few things at home – a reading session and a little number work, tables and daily piano practise, with ten minute breaks between each. Stefan appears to be happy not to be at school. He is frightened of being bullied in secondary school. Today after his 'lessons', he rode his bike for a while. Unbeknown to me, he had ridden round to the local primary school and whilst the children were outside in the playground during their lunch break, he decided to cycle around their grounds. The Head Teacher was called out and she had to ask him to leave the premises. He called her a rude name. I rang to apologise.

September 11th

Stefan decided to repeat yesterday's activity whilst Vaughan was looking after him. This time he rode his bike around the infant school's playing field which is almost next door to us. The Head Teacher of this school came outside and ticked him off. He became verbally abusive. She rang and complained to Vaughan. Vaughan was livid. He made Stefan write a note of apology and frog-marched him round to the school to deliver it personally. 'He won't do that again!' declared Vaughan. Famous last words!

September 12th

Stefan arrived at his former primary school. He rode up and down the pavement outside shouting rude things to the dinner ladies. The deputy Head Teacher rang to let me know about it. More apologies. No bike for a week.

September 28th

Stefan found my blue food colouring in the cupboard. He made himself a bright blue milk drink. Ever so good for hyperactive children!

September 30th

Our nearest secondary school has been instructed to take Stefan by the Department of Education. They are not prepared for him to start, however, until they have met and discussed a programme for him with the behavioural support team. A member of the team is also to visit the school and give a talk on ADHD. Good.

October 1st

Now we *know* that we have flipped! Stefan went to spend a few hours on a farm with a family who have offered us periodic respite care arranged through Social Services. We took him over there recently and met the animals, dogs, sheep, goat, horses, ducks and geese. A lovely place for a hyperactive child to run free. We fell in love with a little dog that reminded us so much of Pepsi. He needed a home. We succumbed again!

October 4th

Stefan has a new obsession. One of the things about those with ADHD is that once an idea gets into their heads they will go on and on about it, refusing to let the subject drop and talking about very little else. This time it's a UNICYCLE. He has decided that he simply must have one.

October 5th

Stefan asked today: 'Mummy, am I a big boy now?'

October 6th

We have a new assistant minister at our church. Stefan recognised him when we were out walking the dogs along the seafront. Without any warning, he left my side, shot across the road and flung himself into his arms. The poor chap looked somewhat confused. He had never even seen Stefan before! I had to go and introduce ourselves but I did not get the opportunity to explain about Stefan. I will do.

October 7th

Stefan was up early. When I arrived home from my weekly 'sleep-in' night duty job, he greeted me with great excitement. 'Mum, mum – guess what? There's been a big burglary. Battersea dog's home has been broken into and all the dogs have escaped!' What had really happened, as I soon found out, was that next door's *car* had been broken into. What imagination!

October 8th

Stefan used very abusive language to our neighbour. The husband came round, hopping mad. Also another neighbour came round later and complained about Stefan. Two in a day! Stefan is now banned from playing near their houses. Vaughan wrote a note of apology. The story of our lives – apologising and attempting to create peace where Stefan has caused chaos.

October 9th

Stefan threw a light bulb onto our patio. At our local swimming pool, we were waiting for Louise, the youngest, to finish her lesson. Stefan found the hose in the changing rooms. He sprayed everybody as they walked by. Then he ran underneath the shower and turned it on whilst fully clothed. Next, he disappeared into a changing cubicle, locked it from the inside and crawled out underneath. Finally, he put his hands around a child's neck because he was 'winding him up'. I could not get out fast enough that night!

October 10th

During this week a film crew arrived to include Stefan in a special report being shown on television about ADHD. Stefan had great fun. The camera man was literally dripping with perspiration running around trying to keep up with him. He said he had never had to work so hard for his money.

October 11th

Stefan has been calling at all the neighbours' houses asking for jumble. He has decided to have another 'shop'. He took our wheelbarrow and came back with many bags full of stuff. He spent ages arranging it all in our dining room, pricing articles up and hanging clothes all around.

October 14th

He has been dragging unsuspecting passers-by into our home to have a look at his 'shop' and hopefully buy something. Nobody gets by our house without an attempted hi-jack by Stefan. As we are a small town, I know most of the people by sight at least, who walk up and down. Stefan also went to our nearby antique shop (without me knowing). He sold a model. He then sold some Gameboy games in our local advertising paper – this time with my help and approval. With the proceeds from his 'shop' and the sales he made, he accumulated enough money to get his unicycle which he had been going on and on about every single day. I had to admire his expertise though. He had seen one in the local bike shop and it was duly ordered and collected the next day. Vaughan and I felt dubious that he would ever learn to ride such a precarious looking machine. To our amazement, he mastered the skill within twenty-four hours! What balance – what skill! He took his unicycle to bed with him!

October 16th

Another neighbour round. Stefan and some other little boys around the corner had been trying to get conkers off a tree. Stefan had picked up a log and slung it up at the tree. It missed and hit a neighbour's window. Fortunately it did not break as it was double-glazed. We explained and apologised and Stefan also said he was sorry. The man went and told the village policeman.

October 17th

Another neighbour came round – an elderly lady. She said Stefan had been rude to her when he came knocking at her door trying to sell postcards that he had got free from the cinema. We banned Stefan from playing in that road.

October 18th

After still hearing nothing about a starting date at school for Stefan, we contacted the Department of Education again. They brought pressure to bear and at last we heard from the school. He is to start the week before half-term, for just a few hours. Stefan was not happy. He had got into a little routine at home and did not want to be disturbed. He was worried and nervous about being bullied and losing his way around the school. I assured him that he would be given plenty of help.

October 21st

Stefan started secondary school at last, after being home for thirteen weeks since July. All the staff had been asked to attend a talk on ADHD by the Behavioural Support Team prior to his admission. All were prepared. Some were apprehensive. Stefan called two girls 'bitches'.

October 23rd

He is finding it hard to settle. Already he is having to spend a day alone tomorrow with the special needs teacher for making suggestive remarks to a girl, who complained. He felt quite despondent when he came out of school, saying he knew it would not work. When he arrived home, he went outside to play for a little while. A neighbour called her children into their house as she did not want them to play with Stefan. That was the final straw for him. He was depressed that night – said he wanted to commit suicide. I felt real heartache for him.

October 24th

We saw one of Stefan's previous school teachers from the primary school coming towards us in her car.

Me: 'There's Mrs B, Stefan. Wave to her.'

Stefan: 'No! She's ugly.'

Me: 'Don't be like that, Stefan. She's very nice.'

Stefan: 'She looks like a walnut!'
(She does, come to think of it!)

October 31st

I was standing on our front door step talking to a neighbour (no, she wasn't complaining about Stefan this time!). When I came back inside the house I nearly choked on some terrible fumes. 'What have you done Stefan?' I demanded. 'Only sprayed "fresh air" with the spray mum,' he meekly replied. I grabbed a half hidden canister. FART SPRAY! I was distracted by the phone ringing. He managed to somehow retrieve the can and proceeded to spray Jane's (my older daughter) face and hair with it before rushing from the house. A few minutes later our next door but one neighbour appeared with clenched fists (thankfully he knows us well and understands our little problem). 'He's just sprayed my wife all over with "fart" spray and she had just put on a clean blouse to go out! Wait till I get hold of him!' he chomped. 'If you catch him before I do,' I replied, 'grab the can and throw it away, please.' This he did, much obligingly.

November 4th

Vaughan had just cleaned an expensive Persian rug for one of his customers. He hung it over our banisters to dry out. Little Stefan decided to make a drink for his Dad. It had the blue food colouring in it. Where do you think he spilled it?!

November 5th

Got up to the most pungent smell of garlic! And cinnamon! Stefan had emptied four bottles of herbs and spices into a bag. He had tried to hide it in his money box! Smell of garlic remained all day. Some child met Stefan in the toy shop today. He told Stefan how to make home-made gunpowder. This child had a bandage on his hand where he had almost blown himself up. Stefan, of course, was fascinated. I heard the words 'vinegar' and 'baking powder' mentioned. I forgot all about it after warning Stefan not to try anything silly or dangerous. One might as well try and tell a dog not to bark. That night I smelt a strong smell of vinegar in his bedroom. Running quickly downstairs and giving my cupboards a hasty check, I found two items missing – vinegar and baking powder! After room search, we finally located the concoction in a plastic bag. Thankfully he must have omitted one important ingredient, whatever it was.

November 6th

Here begins the yearly ritual after bonfire night when Stefan goes around the streets and on to the playing field next door looking for dead fireworks. He lovingly places the blackened, soggy shells into a box and croons over them for the next few days.

November 8th

Took Stefan to Sainsburys. A conveyor belt operates up a slope to the upper car park. Stefan was being very helpful after I finished shopping, offering to push my trolley load to the car park. Although we were parked on the ground level, he just could not resist pushing the trolley onto the conveyor belt which then locks it into position until one reaches the top. I was cross as I had to travel all the way up to the upper car park only to return. I pushed the trolley onto the downward conveyor ready to begin the descent. It locked into position. But the conveyor was not working! I was left standing, red faced and angry, unable to move my trolley an inch. Did I say a few things to Stefan! He had to walk down and fetch the manager, who then had to stop the upward belt and put it in reverse, then somehow unlock my trolley and manoeuvre it on the upward belt which was now moving downwards, whilst streams of heavily laden shoppers patiently stood by, watching the proceedings. I was a very cross Mum that day. (I forgave him, of course!)

November 9th

Attempted some Christmas shopping with Stefan and Louise. It seems such a remarkable coincidence that every time Stefan comes shopping with me and we go into a large department store, the escalators usually break down and stop. Funny that!

November 11th

Stefan seems to be gradually settling into his new school with no major incidents. He has to come home for lunch every day at the moment and I am happy to co-operate with that. Each day, after school I go to his classroom to collect him and have a minute's chat with his class teacher. All seems well at present. What a relief!

November 21st

Stefan came out of school with blue lips. I felt slightly anxious, wondering what had caused it. Until I looked at his hands – INK everywhere!

November 22nd

Stefan's uniform is splattered with Tippex. Who else could get in such a mess? Oh, how he reminds me of the 'Just William' stories!

November 25th

Stefan takes his unicycle everywhere with him. He is extremely adept at riding it now and he enjoys the adulation he receives when he shows off his skills. I wonder what his next obsession will be?!

1997

January 5th

At long last Stefan has been given a statement of special educational needs after five years of battling with the education authorities. This means that his school is allocated funding to provide extra help and classroom support for a set number of hours a week.

Today we went bowling as a family. Stefan was heard to comment to a woman bowling in the next lane, 'Why are you so ugly?' Later on he spotted another woman struggling to bend down and said to her: 'You know, you would be good at bowling if you lost some weight!' At which point Vaughan decided to take a break!

January 8th

Stefan frequently comes out of school black and blue. No he has not been beaten up – he has simply drawn all over his body with marker pen, on his hands, arms, legs, face and knees. He seems to have an attraction for marker pens at present. He writes all over (what is left of) the units in his bedroom, my dressing table, his

Dad's bed-side cabinet, his ceiling and has even written his name on our car's dashboard which is made of vinyl. It is a terrible job to get off and often leaves an indelible print. He continues to come home for lunch every day which I am happy to comply with if it keeps him out of trouble. He has made a few friends and sometimes he will bring one of them home to join us for lunch.

January 9th

Our monthly visit to Great Ormond Street Hospital. Stefan was to be kept off medication so that he could be assessed. Vaughan decided to let me take him as he did not feel able to cope with Stefan 'in the raw'. On the underground train Stefan began to talk to all the passengers around him, introducing people to one another, asking them about their lives, what nationality they were and so on.

By the time we reached our destination, instead of the carriage being in silence with people grimly looking at one another or just minding their own business, there was a low buzz of new conversations. Looking at it positively, I put my arm around Stefan as we stepped off the train. 'You certainly cheer people up, Stefan,' I commented. We climbed into the lift at Russell Square, squashing against each other like sardines. Dead silence. Suddenly Stefan's voice piped up: 'Come on, cheer up everybody!' People smiled at each other and visibly relaxed.

Once at Great Ormond Street, he ran all over the place, darting in and out of rooms, asking questions, not waiting for a reply, and opening cupboards and drawers to investigate. The poor doctor could not keep up with him. His medication was changed after three years on Ritalin.

January 17th

Stefan seemed too quiet on the new medication. Louise remarked on the change; she did not like him so quiet, she wanted the old Stefan back. He seemed TOO normal! His dosage was duly modified and this was much better.

January 18th

Stefan stepped on a wicker shelf in his room. It collapsed. Being ever destructive (or resourceful – I am trying to be positive!) he decided to pull out all the wicker canes and made dozens of bows and arrows. No shelf left, but a wonderful array of weapons!

January 25th

Stefan and a friend got caught knocking on the neighbours' doors and running away. Vaughan was furious.

February 6th

Stefan was playing with his remote control car. He was driving it down the middle of the road despite persistent warnings. I saw a car coming down the road fairly slowly because of the speed humps, thank goodness. At that point, Stefan decided to drive his car across the road. As I looked out of the window, all I saw was the back end of it disappearing under the driver's wheels. I thought it would emerge a mangled heap. By some miracle it somehow avoided being crushed and landed the other side unscathed.

February 7th

Back to Great Ormond Street. Stefan was to be seen on his new medication. The doctor could not believe the difference, as he sat quietly whilst we talked.

February 10th

Stefan appeared in the kitchen with his entire curtain rail with the curtains still on the rail. He had 'had an accident' and it had come right off the wall.

February 11th

My clothes horse went missing. I might have guessed who had it. He had used parcel tape to stick dozens of picture postcards on, supposedly, to 'sell' on the driveway. To give him his due, he had made an ingenious display. He is always trying to find ways of earning money. Our poor neighbours must live on tenterhooks wondering what delights Stefan will try and entice them into buying next. He also carted around many of our videos in the wheelbarrow, hiring them out for a week at a pound a time!

February 18th

A gentleman whom I had never met knocked on our door. Stefan had called his wife a 'cow'. Stefan was made to write a note of apology.

March 1st

Stefan was in church the other day and the choir were giving a joyful and exuberant rendering of a song. Stefan put his hands over his ears during a particularly loud part and called out, 'Oh shut up!'

Just the other day he went up to someone in the street and told them that they looked 'at least a hundred'. It is never-ending.

December 25th

We have had probably the best year so far with Stefan, given the disorder he has. He certainly made up for it this Christmas. We were all at my sister's house celebrating dinner together. My sister brought in the Christmas pudding that she had lovingly made. It looked delicious. She tried to light the brandy that the pudding was swimming in but, try as she might, the brandy would not catch alight. It was not until Christmas and the New Year were well over that we learned the truth. Stefan had gone into her kitchen, tipped the brandy away and replaced it with his urine!

1998

January 1st

Stefan was wakeful and as alert as ever at midnight. He would not come up to bed and was being very lively when we were all shattered. Finally Vaughan snapped and a fracas followed. Nice start to the New Year!

January 2nd

Stefan filled some balloons with Vaughan's shaving foam – they burst all over his quilt cover. He then helped himself to my Christmas hamper that Louise had given me – a whole tin of ham and a pack of apple pies.

January 3rd

Stefan put a rope around his neck and pulled it tighter and tighter until his face started turning purple. I managed to whack it quickly out of his hand. It was well after midnight when he decided to dress himself up in all his 'army' gear. He dragged an old army survival sleeping bag out of a cupboard, found a back pack and transformed his bedroom into an 'army camp'. When we are all winding down, he is winding up!

January 5th

Back to school. Stefan's obsession at the moment is PENS – Parkers! He wheels and deals with anyone and buys them with his pocket money, only to swap them when a nicer looking pen takes his fancy. He swapped four pens for a silver coloured one from a boy at school. His collection stands at about thirty. He is finding it hard to settle down after the holidays and at eleven at night is still getting out of bed 'for a hug'. I had to get very firm with him in the end and tell him 'no more hugs' (he'd had loads!) and put him back to bed.

January 6th

Stefan covered his hands in cochineal after school today – it is semi-permanent. He has taken a fancy to tinned rice pudding and likes to eat a whole tin for supper every night.

January 7th

Stefan hit a boy at school today because the boy called him 'psycho' because Stefan has to take medication. The Head Teacher said it was six of one and half a dozen of the other. Stefan spent the afternoon in isolation and tomorrow he has to do 'litter picking'. At eleven thirty I took Stefan's light bulb out as he was all 'hyped up' and kept switching it on to play. He settled soon after.

January 9th

Stefan had a bath and threw wet tissues rolled up into balls all over the walls where they stuck.

January 10th

He broke all Louise's long pencils in half. Louise was extremely upset. This is another quirk of his, breaking pencils in bits.

January 14th

Stefan called a teacher a rude name at school, so he was kept in for half an hour after school finished to do litter picking and has to do the same again tomorrow.

January 17th

Today half a jacket potato got thrown at the kitchen wall – it splattered all down it and over the carpet. He banged a six inch nail into his bedroom wall.

January 21st

Stefan up until gone midnight. At midnight he splattered blue ink all over the toilet seat and bathroom walls. Has he got an obsession for walls now? He broke a drainpipe at school. I had to write to the Head

Teacher and apologise. Stefan will be in detention on Monday as a result.

January 22nd

Stefan and a friend melted the casing of my hair dryer. WHAT A MONTH!

February 21st

Stefan has become a teenager! We took him to Pizza Hut and unbeknown to him we invited three friends to join us. They were rather late arriving and Stefan became impatient to order his pizza, getting crotchety and demanding. Finally we saw his friends walking up the road and breathed a sigh of relief. Stefan was so delighted to see them and immediately went into 'hyped up' mode, talking loudly and animatedly and generally acting without thinking.

The other boys were no angels either and together made their presence more than felt in the restaurant. I could see that Vaughan was fast reaching that 'I can't stand much more' phase – one look at his eyes and I knew. Sure enough the final straw came when Vaughan visited the gentlemen's toilet. He emerged with his hair almost standing on end and I thought that I would soon see smoke flaring from his nostrils. I tried to ask in a nonchalant manner if there was anything wrong. 'This IS the final straw,' said Vaughan through gritted teeth. 'I've just been clearing up the MESS in the toilets. You should have seen what they have all done!

They'd spat ice-cream all down the walls, and wee'd over the floor. It's time to go.' We left.

On the way back to the car, Stefan must have dropped his wallet containing all the money he had been given for his birthday from the family and his friends at his request. We made extensive enquiries that day and subsequent days and of course reported it to the police, but the money and wallet were never recovered.

February 27th

I now have to hide the toaster as at every opportunity Stefan lights paper or candles or anything else in it.

March 1st

Stefan was very 'high' tonight. He threw a sharp kitchen knife. It stabbed Louise in the leg, almost badly enough to need stitches. He is grounded for the entire week.

March 3rd

Stefan was awake *and* lively until one thirty this morning again, stomping around in his room. I took his light bulb out in the end but later discovered that he had been downstairs and carried the lounge lamp up to his room. This is making us so TIRED.

March 4th

I cannot believe it, but for the third night running Stefan has not settled to sleep until one thirty. We are exhausted. I had remained awake on purpose to try and keep Stefan quiet for Vaughan's sake and remove all available light bulbs. I had just climbed into bed and was dropping off to sleep when I was abruptly woken by the sound of Vaughan's voice shouting at Stefan, which also woke the two girls. Pandemonium!

March 5th

Stefan got up quite lively and was singing at the top of his voice around the house a word that is not appropriate. Vaughan told him to be quiet and ask Mum what it meant. Talk about pass the buck! He changed his song to 'Or–gan–ic, or–gan–ic'.

March 6th

Open evening at his school. Vaughan could not make it so I went alone. There were some positive reports about Stefan from several subject teachers. Felt quite encouraged. Praised Stefan. Later on at home I was hoping that perhaps would get a peaceful night, when Jane suddenly cried out, 'Mum, there's a fire in my bedroom!' I rushed upstairs. She had placed a cloth over a huge glass light dome in her bedroom and it had overheated and caught fire. I had only warned her about it the night before. The whole light fitting was in flames – a lot of them.

I knew that water should not be applied to electrical fires. I rang the fire brigade. Vaughan was still out. I returned to the bedroom. Stefan had found a container and had filled it with water and thrown it up to the ceiling, managing to douse the flames considerably. (We had of course switched the light off immediately.) Stefan was quite remarkable, keeping calm and being very helpful. When the fire brigade arrived a few moments later, everything was under control and Stefan chatted happily to the men, asking them about their job, looking at their uniforms and generally enjoying the excitement. Needless to say, I did not get a quieter or earlier night's sleep!

March 8th

Stefan lit paper and candles in the bathroom and covered the bath in black.

March 9th

Stefan arrived home from the newsagent with a Sport daily newspaper. It was confiscated. Tonight he fixed up Vaughan's extension cable from the garage, plugging it into a lamp and pulled up a drain cover in the pavement. He started digging up the mud in it to get at some old coins that he had buried under there some years back. He found them!

March 10th

Today he covered a quarter of his white bedroom cupboard completely with black marker pen. In doing so, he had also managed to leave a trail of black all over the light switch in the bathroom, basin, soap stand and most of all his hands. It would not come off.

March 16th

A letter arrived from the school. Stefan had defaced an almost new text book and could we please send in a cheque to cover the cost of a new one.

March 20th

The Head of Year came out and met me at the school gate. Stefan had smashed up a school calculator and we would have to pay the cost of a new one. He also told me that Stefan had brought in a lighter to school and had lit it under the desk.

March 23rd

Stefan climbed onto the flat roof outside his bedroom window and threw gravel from the roof all over our driveway.

March 28th

Stefan arrived home with his latest acquisition – a huge tent! He had found it in a garage that he thought was disused. It was covered in dog's mess. Vaughan explained to Stefan why he could not keep it. Stefan was indignant. Vaughan returned it to the garage a few days later, much to Stefan's annoyance.

March 30th

We have to hide all our money because it gets taken. I am running out of hiding places for my handbag.

April 10th

We keep finding lighters in Stefan's bedroom. He seems to be obsessed with matches and lighters and enjoys playing with the flames. It is difficult.

April 11th

Louise was playing at a neighbour's house. Stefan telephoned her there and told her that Dad had had a bad accident and an ambulance was on its way. Louise was understandably distraught, poor child. Later on that day I received a phone call from a shop in the Broadway. Stefan had ridden down there and tried to sell his bike to them. The man wanted to know was he allowed to? I said NO!

April 12th

Stefan threw his friend's bike lock onto a shed housing electricity. His Mum phoned to complain. He came home that afternoon with a bag full of men's ties. 'For you, Dad,' he smiled. Where on earth does he get his stuff from?

Stefan disappeared after church was finished earlier on in the day. He had told us that he was going to the car park to wait in the car. Of course he was not there when it was time to leave. After a search we went into a local shop who said that Stefan had been in and tried to buy lighter fuel. The shopkeeper had refused to serve him, thank goodness. He had then wandered round to some other shops trying to find someone else to serve him so that he could fill up yet another lighter he had somehow got hold of.

April 14th

Today we had a trapeze swing hanging from the rafters in the attic. It is a good thing we are not house proud! A couple of days later, Stefan climbed into the attic again and decided to make a den up there, moving all our carefully stored suitcases and other items onto the rafters.

April 18th

Stefan disappeared for hours. I was beginning to get very worried when Vaughan received a phone call from him saying that he was down at the old part of town, on the sea front, with his friend who is rather similar to Stefan in what he gets up to. The pair of them together are a walking disaster. Vaughan went to look for them. Eventually he found them. They were completely covered from head to foot in MUD – hair, face, trainers and Stefan's brand new yellow coat. He had also taken Jane's bike down onto the mud flats and it, too, was completely caked in thick mud. The bike chain had to be renewed at the cycle shop and, after three washes in the machine, the clothes were still not clean from the debris of mud.

April 19th

Found half a dozen lighters in Stefan's room which he said he had found on the beach yesterday. All were full of lighter fuel.

In church tonight, Stefan made paper aeroplanes out of the notice sheets and flew them across the pews during the sermon. He then chewed up pieces of paper, took them out of his mouth and flicked them all over the floor in little bits. Finding that boring after several minutes he then tied his shoe lace, with his foot still in the shoe, to the pew. After the service was over he walked down the aisle with both feet tied together after trying to grab the communion glass from me and dipping his finger in the wine.

April 20th

Stefan 'peanutted' a teacher's tie at school today. Apparently this means yanking the tie extremely hard, causing it to tighten. The trouble was it was still on the teacher! Stefan was put in isolation the next day.

April 21st

Stefan swore at a neighbour. The husband came round and gave me a mouthful. I felt very upset. After an hour or so, giving time for emotions to cool, I decided the best thing was to go round and speak to them and not be defensive but explain a bit about Stefan and to apologise. I felt very nervous, especially as the man had spoken so aggressively. They let me go in, and I explained as best I could. They were very understanding and we left each other on much better terms. It seems that I am forever trying to build bridges and make peace with irate neighbours!

April 24th

Stefan has found out that he can ring freephone numbers and either leave messages on answerphones or speak directly to someone at the other end of the line. Despite being severely reprimanded, it makes no difference. We have had a code put on the phone but these freephone numbers are exempt.

April 26th

Stefan cooked bacon in quite a lot of oil in the frying pan. When he had finished cooking he tipped the hot oil over the fence into the next door neighbour's garden.

April 27th

He tipped a packet of two hundred rubber bands into his bath at ten o'clock at night.

April 29th

He tipped about two hundred and fifty foreign coins into his bath at ten o'clock at night.

April 30th

He tried to light his 'army' belt in the bathroom to see if it was flammable. The bathroom was filled with smoke.

May 2nd

He burned paper towels in the toaster. The kitchen was full of smoke.

May 3rd

He found the master key to our local church and was seen trying to get into the side door.

May 4th

I took Stefan, Louise and a friend of each to a Western Fayre out in the country. On the journey, Stefan produced his magnifying glass from his pocket and spent the entire time trying to burn holes in his jeans by training the magnifying glass onto the material whilst reflecting the strong sunlight. I was constantly distracted by this, especially when I saw smoke starting to rise from his trouser leg. He found a pipe during the afternoon and sucked on it intermittently despite my admonitions that it was full of germs and had probably belonged to some dirty old dribbly man.

Stefan covered the car with hay whilst I was parked at the fayre and all the way home bits of hay were flying out from under the windscreen or sun roof where it had been wedged. When we arrived home, a neighbour saw us and asked Stefan what he did at the fayre. 'Met a prostitute!' came the reply.

May 6th

Stefan went out for a while with his friend. Later the friend told me that Stefan had been lying down in the road where some road works were taking place.

May 9th

It was such a glorious day that I decided to take the children on the beach. There is a bowling green on one side of the pathway. Stefan threw a water bomb onto the green where there was a bowling match in full swing. He threw stones and mud, and on the way home he chucked a toy car out of the window. I have to watch him all the time like a toddler as he is usually up to something. It is not very restful. He seems to have so little social awareness.

May 10th

Stefan and a friend from the next road decided to flood our garden patio with the hosepipe, blocking off the drainage. They were making their own 'paddling pool'. They spent about an hour filling up the slight incline with the hose, buckets of water and anything else they could find which held water. They rolled up their jeans and paddled about in great glee. Oh well, harmless enough for once – at least it kept them GOOD!

May 16th

Stefan decided that a repeat run of this activity would be fun. I saw the patio slowly filling up with water. What I did not know was that, in addition to using our hose, he had gone round to our neighbour's house whilst they were out, found their hose and had run it over our fence to aid the filling up process.

May 17th

Perhaps it was not such a good idea of harmless fun after all. The boy from the next road was here again, and guess what they decided to do? Vaughan had had enough. He threw a wobbler and stormed out of the house for the next few hours. The boys paddled on.

May 18th

Stefan is fixated on the hose. The neighbour on the other side was about to unpeg her dry washing when her telephone rang and she ran indoors to answer it. Meanwhile Stefan decided to drench her washing with the hose. I did not hang around to watch the outcome, coward that I am! A little while later, our neighbour on the other side knocked on our door. Had I by any chance seen the nozzle of her hosepipe? OH NO!!

May 20th

At eleven o'clock at night, I discovered the sweet little boy had covered his arms, hands and legs in OIL paints. We only had a tiny drop of white spirit left in the garage and somehow we had to clean him up. It was difficult and I was *not* amused.

May 21st

Found Stefan lying in bed in a wartime gas mask!

June 10th

I had been given a set of three photo albums for my birthday. Stefan found them and broke the seal, using them for his coin collection. He thinks that whatever he fancies is there for the taking.

June 11th

He had a 'shop' on the front driveway of our house. This is one of his favourite activities, even though we do not like him selling things from our house. He sold some of his video games and made himself fifty pounds.

June 13th

Stefan has a new obsession – tennis! At last, something ordinary! He wants to play every day with anyone and everyone who is willing to give him a game. He is quite good and it warms my heart to see him doing a sport and enjoying it so much. Vaughan has started to play as well and I love seeing the two of them go off to the courts dressed in their whites.

June 23rd

I asked Stefan to go and brush his teeth. Instead, he picked up his tennis racket and whacked it in the air, accidentally smashing his whole light fitting and fusing all the upstairs lights. We were not happy!

June 24th

Dared to join Stefan up with a tennis club. It is the first club he will be part of since he was quite young, as no club kept him. I do hope that he does not blow his chances.

June 30th

Early days still but an encouraging letter received from the owner of the tennis club. Stefan is doing really well, showing great promise and fitting in. Hallelujah!

July 10th

Picked Stefan up from his music lesson. He got into the car. I wound the window down to have a word with his teacher about something. Before I could say a word, Stefan leaned across me and called out to his teacher, who, I may say, is an extremely gentle and pleasant lady: 'Mrs. ...., you are an insult to a pig!' 'Stefan!' I hissed, 'What are you saying?' He clapped his hand over his mouth. 'Oh, I'm sorry, I did not mean to say that,' he quickly replied. He looked rather ashamed of himself this time. This unpremeditated behaviour is so typical of children with an attention deficit disorder. It is as if a filter is missing between thought and action.

August 3rd

Stefan climbed up into our attic and *drilled* a hole through into our bedroom ceiling. He drilled another hole through to the landing. He also got out all the old photographs that had been carefully stored in suitcases from my grandmother, and made a huge mess with them all over the attic, using the now empty cases for his own 'antiques'.

August 7th

Went to visit some cousins of mine some twenty miles away. We had a pleasant afternoon. When we arrived home, they rang. They were really sorry to bother me but they noticed that a tiny silver antique pill box had gone missing from a small table and did I know where one of the children could have put it. I found it – in Stefan's pocket!

August 17th

Visited my uncle and aunt's cottage in Derbyshire. The place is adorned with antiques and valuable pictures on the walls, exquisite ornaments and plates, trinkets and other fascinating items collected over the years from their stays abroad. Stefan took it all in. Thereby began the trigger for a new obsession – PLATES! The next day I discovered his bedroom had been carefully decorated with old plates, cups and saucers arranged along the window sills, shelves and any available space to make it look like the old cottage he had so admired.

August 20th

Stefan goes around the neighbourhood knocking on doors, asking for any jumble. He arrives home with old PLATES, pictures, cups and saucers.

August 21st

Stefan keeps arranging and re-arranging his room to accommodate all the plates, saucers and cups that he is fast acquiring. They are EVERYWHERE – on shelves, window ledges, desk tops – there hardly seems an area where there is not a plate. Harmless, I suppose, and a lot better than some of the things that he has done in the past.

August 25th

Took Stefan to the Broadway where we went round every single second-hand and charity shop. He bought a whole collection of old plates!

August 28th

Traipsed around a market of antique stalls with him, looking for old plates again. He picks each one up to read the writing underneath and is quickly learning which ones have a value on them. He is learning the names like Royal Doulton, Wedgwood, Royal Worcester, and so on. Stefan still learns best by 'hands on' and visual stimuli. I would not be surprised if he does end up in the antiques business one day!

August 30th

We all went on a sponsored walk with our local ADHD support group. Stefan met with other ADHD children. He got very 'high' and made a lot of inappropriate comments to passers-by.

August 31st

Took Stefan to North Essex to an antiques fair. He examined the underside of many plates. He took a bag of plates that he no longer wanted and tried to flog them to the antique dealers. To no avail. When we got home he organised a 'boot sale' on our front lawn. Louise got involved with this. She sold her lovely dolls pram for a tenner and Stefan sold a pogo stick for a fiver. They felt very satisfied with themselves.

September 3rd

Stefan disappeared down the road on his bike. I just caught a glimpse of him with a full size 'fly-mo' lawn mower somehow slung over his back. Ours! I prayed for his safety – I knew that I would not be able to catch up with him and I guessed where he was going – to an old lady's house not very far away. Sure enough he returned some while later and asked me to go and pick up the mower from her garden. 'I've done as best as I could with her front lawn,' Stefan told me. I praised him for such a kind gesture. The only trouble was he had completely broken the mower – it was unusable. It set us back over seventy pounds to replace it!

September 4th

This is a resume of what Stefan did during this particular evening: He managed to break my china toilet roll holder in the bathroom. He threw dried mud and earth through Jane's window covering her bed, shelves, covers and carpet. He was sent into the bathroom to have a bath. When he finally emerged, he had glued all over the toilet seat and stuck toilet paper on top of it. He had put glue all over the door handles and had put glue inside Louise's bedroom door lock and on the handle. Vaughan flipped.

September 5th

Vaughan and I went out for a meal with some friends, a fairly infrequent occurrence as it is difficult to get baby-sitters. I wonder why?! My sister looked after Louise and Stefan at her house and had invited my parents up for some games. Stefan was very 'high' all evening. He used language to shock and in the end my father became irate and threatened to go home.

September 6th

Stefan squirted thick white bathroom cleaner all over the bathroom window sill, ledges and even on Louise's desk. He had also squirted the stuff over our neighbour's adjacent landing window. They put a note through our door – would we go round and see them tomorrow?

September 7th

Had to go round to next door neighbours and apologise for what Stefan had squirted onto their window. Dragged Stefan round to apologise too. They were NOT amused.

September 11th

Stefan threw talcum powder all over the bathroom. I made him hoover it up.

September 14th

Stefan abseiled down the banisters, taking off large chunks of paint and wood. I've had to give up any hopes of having a smart house for the immediate future.

September 15th

Stefan keeps spraying deodorant everywhere, all over doors, shelves and the walls. He has worked his way through two canisters in two weeks. I have now bought roll-on deodorants and explained why to Vaughan.

September 17th

The TV cameras came to film Stefan and me for part of a television documentary programme. Stefan climbed onto next door's roof.

September 21st

Large collection bags were left in people's letter boxes in our area for the Heart Foundation. Stefan went around the roads with a wheelbarrow collecting the bags that had been filled with clothes and other items from people, telling them that the Heart Foundation had sent him as their van had broken down. An enormous amount of stuff was collected which he put in our garage. He then proceeded to price all the things and put them up for sale on our driveway.

We discovered their origin when one suspicious lady took the trouble to phone us up and check on Stefan's story. Vaughan was furious and I was pretty upset. We spent the next half hour bagging all the stuff up again and putting the bags back out for the authentic lorry to collect the following day. Stefan was grounded for a week.

September 27th

Went to my sister's chalet in Kent for the weekend. Stefan wee'd in the cash tray of a fruit machine there. He threw Louise's shorts up high in the swimming pool and they caught on to a hanging plant. We had to leave them there.

September 28th

Stefan picked runner beans from the next door neighbour's plant and brought them into the kitchen. I was horrified when I discovered where they came from. They have had such a packet full from Stefan's antics. I was even more horrified when I went outside and saw their runner bean plants – they had built a small trellis just the other side of our fence and had grown just enough for the two of them. There were hardly any left!

This time I did not have the heart to go and show them what Stefan had done; I sort of hoped they would not notice or that a few more would quickly grow! I could not use them myself somehow, so after a week or so I threw them in the bin. I never did hear from the neighbours this time. Maybe they thought there were some hungry animals around!

October 5th

Stefan called a teacher something very rude. He was put into detention for the week.

October 7th

Stefan swore at another teacher.

October 9th

Stefan chews Rizla papers. He has taken to pulling the inside part of a biro out and blowing these chewed up papers through the empty pen holders. There are blobs of paper all over the walls and ceiling.

October 11th

On week days I normally go into Stefan's bedroom to wake him up by announcing 'tablet time' to which he opens his mouth and I drop his tablets in before he is hardly awake. During the church service this morning, Stefan found my sweeteners in my handbag. He took one out and tried to stuff it into my mouth. 'Tablet time,' he declared.

October 14th

Stefan is being kept in for detention almost every day at the moment. This is for not completing homework, forgetting equipment, or misbehaviour in some way. It is quite disconcerting. He even skived off a detention the other day. Somehow I feel that Stefan and other children with ADHD respond better to positive reinforcement than to homing in on the negative aspects of their behaviour. Although it is difficult in a school where they cannot be seen to be getting away with things. It poses quite a challenge to staff, let alone the parents of such children.

Stefan often takes articles into school that do not invite a positive response. He found a Swiss army knife and took it in. The other day he decided to take a hot water bottle in, filled up, of course, with hot water. When questioned, he replied matter-of-factly to the teacher: 'Well, it's a cold day. I've brought it in to keep warm!' Of course!

October 30th

I attended an ADHD conference in London. It was excellent. On the last day, ADHD teenagers were invited to a day's seminar of their own. How brave of the organisers, I thought. Stefan made some choice remarks to conference guests and even to some of the ordinary hotel guests there. Between them they caused mayhem.

October 31st

Our poor neighbours were Stefan's target for more antics yet again. This time a whole tray of soiled cat litter got emptied over their front garden. Another letter of complaint through our letter box. Who can blame them?

After firework night is over Stefan is usually quite obsessed with bonfires. As predicted, he built a bonfire after school on our back patio. He spent a long time hunting for wood and sticks, in fact anything that could be burned. He took the wheelbarrow around the neighbourhood and piled it up with anything burnable. The bonfire was built larger and even some large planks of wood were carefully propped up all ready to be lit.

When Vaughan arrived home from work the fire was lit and for a long while father and son sat outside watching the flames dancing in the shadows, joined by Louise cuddled up on a blanket. It looked a happy scene. It was not until the next day that we heard that Stefan had nicked some wooden ramps belonging to a family in the next road and used them for his bonfire!

November 9th

Stefan has another three days' detention for various misdemeanours – all things typical of an ADHD child with poor self-regulation. The class teacher also expressed his concern that Stefan was not turning up for registration at the end of each day before going out of school. Thinking back to what I had learned at the recent conference I had attended, I suggested using positive reinforcement to encourage him to attend. The idea was to use coupons signed by the teacher which would be given to Stefan each day that he turned up for registration. These could be traded in for a small reward by me at the end of each completed week. The teacher embraced the idea favourably.

November 11th

Picked Stefan up at lunchtime as usual. On the way home I noticed something flapping out of the corner of my eye. Stefan had found a cassette tape at the school gate and had unravelled it and was flying it out of the car window, leaving a long trail behind us.

Tonight I was out and Vaughan in charge. I arrived home quite late to find all four of them still up. What a sight greeted my eyes when I went upstairs! Stefan had cut his bedroom carpet and underlay in half and rolled it up. He had pulled the pine panelling off his wall above the door along with the coving in that area. He had dismantled nearly all of his furniture and parked the bits all around the upstairs and had cleared his ornaments and dozens of collected plates, packing them into any available space upstairs.

In fact, his entire room, apart from his bed and a cupboard, had been stripped. He had even taken down his light fitting and tried to fix up some old contraption that he had bought for fifty pence at a church auction, completely taking a risk with the wiring and ruining the light and circuit and requiring an electrician's visit the next day. What on earth had warranted such drastic action? I questioned Stefan to try and understand his motive. 'I'm going to decorate my room' was his reply. In his mind he had decided that he wanted to change his room and have it decorated. Therefore his thoughts drove him to act on impulse without regard for the consequences.

November 14th

I went out Christmas shopping with Jane today. What chaos I returned to again! Stefan had decided to make a tropical bathroom. He had taken all the plants from around the house – real, silk or dried, and hung them from strategic places such as the shower head, the shower rail, the window sill, and the toilet cistern. There were plants everywhere. He had arranged all his 'army' gear around, dangling from every available space and had filled the bath tub with water and earth. 'It's for you,' he smiled.

I smiled back through gritted teeth. 'Lovely, very imaginative, but it has to be cleared up now.' I struggled to control myself. He sensed my impatience. I was also weary of all this and besides, we were expecting visitors that evening. I'd had enough. 'Will you clear it up now, please, Stefan,' I repeated. He lost his temper and sprinkled half a tin of talcum powder around the bathroom. He then smashed an ornament of Louise's which she had recently bought at some boot sale. She cried loudly and furiously.

To try and let him know how it felt, I took one of his many plates off his shelf, one with no worth, and broke it. So he picked up another three of his plates and smashed them all over the kitchen floor, then pulled Louise's hair. I should not have done it but I was feeling so fraught that day that my feelings got the better of me. Later that evening after our friends had gone home, I felt tired and fairly despondent as I cleared up yet another dreadful mess.

November 17th

Stefan cut all the 'eyes' off Vaughan's fishing rod to make a kite pole. Vaughan was livid.

November 21st

Tonight I came home to an 'old-fashioned' kitchen! All my appliances had been packed in cupboards to overflowing. Packets of pasta, rice and dried beans had been opened and tipped into bowls for 'displays'. A candle had been lit on the table and everything rearranged. I must admit that there was some finesse to the finished room. Nevertheless, I am wondering which room he is going to tackle next when I am out. Perhaps I had better not go out any more!

November 28th

Stefan bought three early twentieth century pictures from a bazaar that I took the children to. He paid fifty pence for them. Later on that day he went to the Broadway shops and sold his pictures for fifteen pounds!

November 29th

Vaughan took Stefan to a huge antiques centre. Stefan bought a pile of old postcards from a dealer for a pound. He went next door to another unit and flogged the postcards to the dealer for three times as much as he had paid! Is this the sign of a shrewd business man? The dealers at this antiques centre all seemed to know Stefan as he has visited on quite a few occasions, and they always greet him very affably. I wonder if they would if they knew what he was up to?!

November 30th

After some deliberation, we have decided to drop one of Stefan's tablets at lunchtime to see if it makes any difference to him at bedtime as he is so wakeful and alert until the early hours often and then cannot get up in the morning for school. He is now falling asleep between eleven and twelve thirty at night instead of about one o'clock; not a lot of difference. The trouble is that his behaviour has deteriorated during the evenings, which sometimes drives us to distraction and the girls to despair. We seem to be caught in a catch twenty-two situation.

December 3rd

When I returned from my usual Thursday evening church night, I was greeted with the now to be expected mayhem. Stefan had dismantled my large lounge picture that was hanging on our wall to get at the frame for his own use. Two other frames had likewise been dismantled. He had decided to frame some very old family portraits from an album belonging to my late grandmother that we had specifically told him not to touch. He had dropped the glass of one of the frames and it had smashed all over his bedroom floor. Vaughan was at his wits' end again. It was the last thing he wanted to deal with after a hard day's work. Louise could not get to sleep because of all the shouting and I felt like walking right back out again!

December 6th

We awoke to Stefan being completely 'over the top'. He was using my parcel tape to put round everything in sight, throwing things around, giggling inanely and being totally out of control. I shoved his tables down him as fast as I could but it was one of those days when his medication seemed of little consequence. I felt absolutely at my wits' end, ready to snap completely. All day long it continued, with him hurling himself around, being silly and annoying everyone.

December 7th

I found our china soap dish broken in the bathroom today. Then I discovered that the shelf over our bed had been snapped. Stefan admitted both 'accidental' crimes. Our house is slowly being depleted of anything nice.

December 9th

Stefan's review at school with regard to his statement. Vaughan and I attended along with the Head of Year, the Educational Psychologist, the Special Needs Co-ordinator and two careers advisors. And Stefan. New targets were set for the forthcoming weeks and difficulties and progress talked through and discussed. Vaughan and I feel that Stefan needs a lot more one-to-one support in class as he is under-achieving and his impulsivity gets him into a lot of trouble with certain teachers who are not used to dealing with a child with attention deficit disorder. They are gradually becoming more familiarised and aware of his difficulties but we always feel that we have to push the education authorities to get the desired help. It is an ongoing battle, for want of a better word.

Tonight I went to my dance class for one hour. When I got back the house was in uproar. Stefan had completely disrupted everyone. Vaughan was beside himself and Louise was crying and saying her life was ruined. Stefan ended up taking a swipe at Louise in bed who screamed and cried in a distraught manner. Vaughan was in danger of going completely mental so I had to take over and try to calm them all down. Every time I go out I wonder what I will come home to. Now that we have lowered the dosage of his tablets a little, Stefan is more strung up and things have intensified negatively during the evenings. But we also need our sleep and he does too and when he was on the higher dosage our day did not end until sometimes the early hours of the morning. He has taken to moving things about, swapping things over in the house, emptying tins, holders or other containers and filling them up with different things, like my cleaners or my herbs or anything else that takes his fancy. It is costing so much extra from my weekly housekeeping to have to replace what he constantly uses up.

December 10th

Tonight he had filled up my ornamental weighing scales with some strong smelling liquid mixture. He'd made another concoction in one of my storage jars.

December 13th

I took Stefan to the antiques centre again where all the unit holders greet him amicably and cheerfully with 'And what have you bought for us to see today, Stefan?' He passes from stall to stall, from unit to unit, until he finds someone interested and willing enough to buy one or two items of his that he has picked up from a charity shop or bazaar. Today he wheeled and dealed and came away eleven pounds better off than when he first arrived. He was very satisfied.

December 14th

I made Stefan tidy his room with me today after school amidst loud protests that went on constantly from start to finish. It took an hour and during that time he became more and more irate and aggressive in his attitude because I insisted he finished the job with me. Most of his stuff had to be thrown out to the rubbish as he had dismantled so much. A cheap second-hand computer had to be thrown out along with a monitor and printer that he had taken apart. He carried the heavy monitor downstairs and outside to the rubbish. Minutes later I heard a loud, continuous banging and rushed downstairs to find him bashing the monitor screen with the garden spade!

December 15th

Stefan made an ingenious contraption – a box strapped onto Vaughan's golf trolley which in turn was somehow fixed behind his bike. He filled the box with videos and went around the neighbourhood 'renting' our videos for a pound a time. Fortunately no-one wanted any, much to his disappointment and to our relief!

December 16th

Stefan takes part in a badminton class each week. Tonight I stayed to watch. He was playing with one of the coaches. I was greatly impressed. Stefan has become a very good player, and with his quick reactions could reach some shots that no-one else could. He played a game of expertise. This skill has not come about by chance. About three years ago, Stefan went to some children's holiday activities. He disrupted the classes each time he went until the supervisors told me that for safety reasons he would not be allowed to go during any other school holidays, the story of our lives.

However, one coach, a lady who ran the badminton part of the activities, saw things in a different light, and was not willing to give up on him and discard him along with the rest. Vaughan and I bless the day we ever met her. She told us to bring Stefan along to her sessions and she would take responsibility for him and face the consequences. She saw beyond the problem, she saw a child who had potential and she was determined to do something about it.

She began to teach him the skills on a one-to-one basis. This continued for a long time. Over the months, she gradually introduced first one player, then another and another until Stefan could play with her, in a foursome. It took a lot of time and a lot of patience and skilful handling of situations on her part. She never once gave up on him. She believed in him and learned when to divert his attention when he was becoming bored with one activity. He learned to love this lady and rewarded her efforts by responding to her careful coaching. What a joy it was to watch the result of the past three years and to see how well he played and handled being in a class of people. How much we owe this wonderful lady who has done so much for him, and purely from the kindness of her heart. She is one of those 'one-in-a-million' people!

December 18th

School's out for Christmas! All the children swarmed out of school, some eager to get home, others tarrying, some with their hair or person decorated with tinsel, all looking happy and relieved that another term was over.

No sign of Stefan. As I sat and waited, and waited, watching the school gates for his familiar little figure, the head teacher approached me. Stefan was being kept in for detention. Could I come back later? As I drove away, I felt so sad that even on the last day of term, he was prevented from leaving with all the other kids. I wondered why he could not have fulfilled his detention during the day; still, mine not to argue.

December 19th

Vaughan went off to Somerset with Louise to visit his parents and take the Christmas presents to them. I took Stefan to a paintballing centre. Set amidst acres of woodland, the young people fire pellets of paintballs at each other after they are divided into war teams. They spend the day playing a number of games after tuition is given and outfits supplied. Stefan had been looking forward to this day. His big sister, Jane, had bravely volunteered to go with him as he could not find a friend to accompany him.

I left them at nine o'clock in the morning on a bright, crisp and cold day. When I picked them up, they were hardly recognisable, so covered with mud were they. They peeled off the outfits that had been supplied. Stefan had somehow got himself covered in mud UNDER his outfit and all over his face. Then I looked at his shoes. They were unrecognisable! It was not until we got into the car and he had taken them off that I realised with horror that he had worn his SCHOOL shoes!

December 21st

Only four days left until Christmas and almost the end of yet another year. And so our story goes on. Undoubtedly there will be more incidents and more adventures ongoing with our mischievous, funny, frustrating, challenging and adorable son. We will have new challenges to face as he grows into his teen years and new things to learn. We will no doubt have more heartaches, more tears and more laughter with him. One thing is certain. We will never, ever stop loving him. We will always be there for him, no matter what.

ADHD

ADHD is not a new condition. It was first described nearly one hundred years ago, and has been diagnosed and treated for over forty years. It is a strongly hereditary condition, boys being more often affected than girls. It is caused by structural and chemical differences in the brain. The condition is usually split into two categories – ADHD which is when hyperactivity is present and ADD where it is not. The symptoms are usually apparent before the age of six. Characteristics include:

- Hyperactivity

- Fidgety – squirms in seat, taps with hands or feet constantly (adolescents may feel always restless or 'on edge')

- Shifts from one activity to another – leaves things uncompleted

- Difficulty remaining seated when required to do so

- Difficulty remaining on task – easily bored

- Highly intrusive behaviour

- Extremely impulsive – acts before thinking

- Excitability

- Aggressive behaviour

- Disruptive behaviour

- Difficulty awaiting turn in group or games situations

- Difficulty playing quietly

- Irritable/short-tempered

- Very short attention span – easily distracted

- Very demanding of attention – extremely persistent – does not give up easily when wanting something

- Often engages in physically dangerous activities without thought for the consequences

- Extremely disorganised and untidy – often loses things necessary for tasks at home or school

- Limited self-awareness – insensitive to the reaction of others

- Very poor social awareness – often the class 'clown', lacks friends

- Inappropriate verbal exchange – blurts out answers to questions before they have been completed, monopolises discussions, butts in on conversations

- Excessive talking – does not appear to listen to instructions

- Often does not appear to have heard what is being said to him/her – brain otherwise engaged or distracted

- Poor eye contact and/or motor regulation

- Poor sleep patterns
- Often underachieves academically despite being usually intelligent and bright
- Anxious quest for intense stimulation or a 'buzz'
- Seeks instant gratification.

Of course, everyone displays many of these characteristics at times and in varying measure, but with ADHD sufferers the behaviours are the 'norm' rather than the exception. They do not respond when disciplined and the behaviours are very severe and can occur in any situation. The hallmark of ADHD is a lack of self-regulation. Children with ADHD may take up to ten times longer to learn to self-regulate than the ordinary child. They do not learn from their mistakes. These children do not set out to be like this, they are biologically driven. Often there are co-existing conduct and oppositional disorders.

Help

Most experts agree that a multi-modal approach aimed at helping the whole child is needed using a combination of behavioural management programmes, medications, educational interventions and parental training. It is very important to work with building on their strengths and raising their usually poor self-esteem, which is often quite difficult when the behaviour is particularly challenging. Locating positive aspects is an important and integral part of their development.

For those parents who have a child whom they suspect may have ADHD an initial visit to their local GP is essential.

From there, a referral to a specialist or to a clinic specialising in attention disorders may be appropriate. ADHD may be a lifelong disorder requiring lifelong help and assistance. The children and their families need continual understanding and support.

Medication

Medication may not be suitable for all children with ADD/ADHD. In certain cases the proper use of medication can play an important and integral part in the child's overall treatment, especially where the child's behaviour is seriously affected both at home and at school.

Appendix

Recommended Reading

The Hyperactive Child. Dr Eric Taylor

The Hidden Handicap. Dr Gordon Serfontein. Simon and Schuster (Australia)

Is My Child Hyperactive? Jo Douglas

The ADHD Parenting Handbook. Colleen Alexander-Roberts

Understanding ADHD Dr Christopher Green

For further information contact:

ADD Information Services

P.O. Box 340

Edgware

London HA8 9HL

Fax 0181 386 6466

Web site *www.adiss.co.uk*

A full list of UK support groups is available. Also books and videos available from the above address.

ADD/ADHD Family Support Group UK

Send s.a.e. to:
Gill Mead
1a High Street
Dilton Marsh
Westbury
Wiltshire BA13 4DL

Teresa Conway

2a Millers Lane
Stanway
Colchester
Essex CO3 5PS
Tel 01206 767603

ADD/ADHD County Support Essex

Kim Allen
9 Fraser Close
Shoeburyness
Essex SS3 9YT
Tel 01702 290840

Parentline National Office

(Helpline for parents)
Endway House
Endway
Hadleigh
Benfleet
Essex SS7 2AN
Tel 01702 559900
Freephone: text phone 0800 736783
Fax 01702 554911